7 Levers of Great Managers

Mastering the Skills of Leadership Success

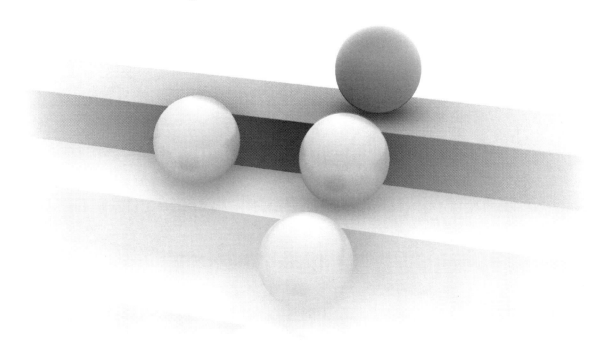

7 Levers of Great Managers

Mastering the Skills of Leadership Success

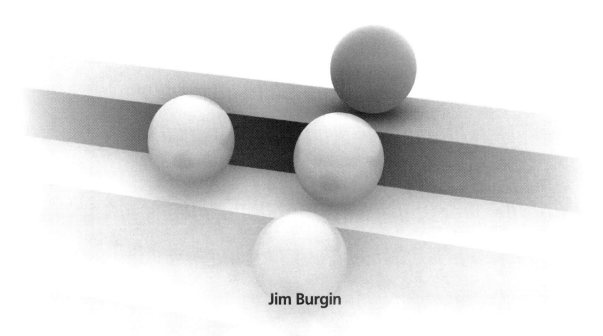

Jim Burgin

SkillPath® Publications

Editor: Bill Cowles

Cover design: Jason Sprenger

Layout: Barbara Hartzler

ISBN: 978-19345892-5-0

Printed in the United States of America

Table of Contents

Foreword

"Give me a place to stand on and I will move the earth."

—Archimedes (287 – 212 BC)

In every field there are people who rise to the level of greatness. They have not been content with "good enough." They have not been satisfied to become caretakers of the way things are. They want to make a lasting contribution that makes a difference. You may be such a person.

Out of Russia comes a story of a monk who is walking down a snow-covered road. As he makes a turn, a soldier steps out of the forest, points a rifle and demands answers:

"Who are you?"
"Where are you going?"
"Why do you want to go there?"

The monk thinks for a moment, then responds:

"How much does the army pay you?"

The soldier is taken aback. He is not accustomed to people asking him questions when he is the one holding the rifle. But, collecting his wits, he replies:

"Two hundred a month."

The monk then takes the soldier to a new place in which he begins to think about his life in much the same way that the monk does:

"I will pay you three hundred a month if you will meet me on this same road, at this same time, every day, and ask me those same three questions."

Who are you? Where are you going? Why?

There is not enough management talent around. If you will take the trouble to prepare, extraordinary opportunities to influence, contribute and reap personal satisfaction will come your way. Where are you going?

Great managers have learned that there are levers that render their efforts more influential. The principle of the lever that Archimedes explained two centuries before Christ is worthy of a manager's attention: *Given a place to stand, a lever and a fulcrum to rest the lever on, it is possible to move objects that would otherwise be too heavy to move.*

Leverage is a concept from mechanics. It says that a given amount of effort can become more powerful by the use of a lever. A heavy weight that would be impossible to move can be moved by using of a lever.

Archimedes, widely regarded as the most influential scientist in antiquity, didn't invent the lever, but he gave the first robust explanation of its power to increase the effectiveness of human effort. He showed how and why a lever would move objects that would otherwise be too heavy to move. Though not schooled in modern management, he explained a principle that is relevant: Nothing can make success in management simple, quick or easy. But here you will find:

- The timeless body of **knowledge** that supports the practice of management as one fad passes away and the next takes the stage

- Pathways to **skill** enhancement

- Open doors to self-knowledge and **attitudes** that make all the difference

Management is heavy lifting. Companies and organizations have a weightiness born in their history, nurtured in their inertia and confirmed in their successes. But in the 21st century, even past success must be leveraged higher. Powerful competition, globalization, the prevalence of the knowledge worker in the workforce, technology and a rapidly changing marketplace all require that managers leverage their companies up the scale of efficiency and effectiveness. This is now as true for a public service organization as for a private business enterprise.

Effectiveness is getting what you and your organization need and want in a way that allows you to get it again and again. Great managers do that by using seven levers:

1. They develop their personal ability to influence

2. They manage themselves, their priorities, communication, time, anxieties and style

3. They integrate leadership into their management

4. They facilitate the life-cycle of employees

5. They establish accountability

6. They align groups, teams and the company

7. They lead change

This book is a guide to reflection on your practices. Don't rush through it. Reflect. Ponder. What made that last meeting go so well? How did it happen that the project launched in such hope came unraveled? At the end of each chapter are suggested steps you can take to leverage what you have learned into practice.

The principles and skills we will discuss will leverage your success, helping you take it to the next level, whether you are managing a for-profit business, a not-for-profit organization or a government agency.

Skill in the use of these levers is learned, not inborn. This book presents what I have learned across a career in management, training, consulting and coaching. The personal stories from consulting and coaching are drawn from my experience. They are real but have been altered to preserve the anonymity of my clients.

You are still writing your story. When you finish your career in management, others will add the final sentences …

"I'll tell you something, when he was a manager here … "

"You always knew that she would … "

"You could count on him to … "

"What we accomplished when she was the leader was … "

"I learned … "

"Looking back on that time, I feel … "

Come along. Write on! Get your hands on seven levers that make all the difference. Success and personal satisfaction await you.

—Jim Burgin

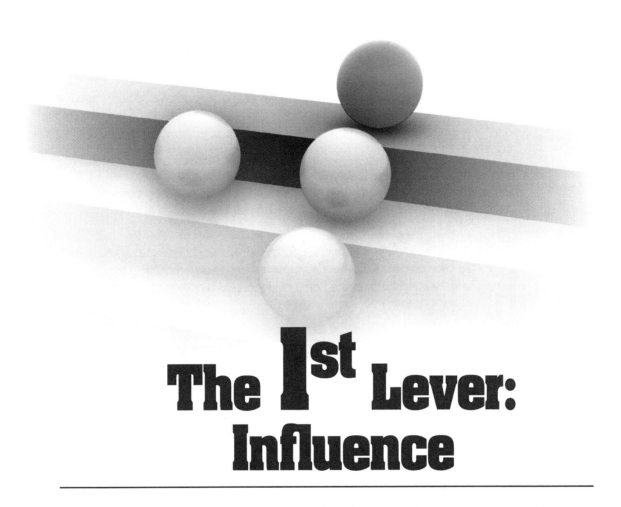

The 1st Lever: Influence

Whether you're new to management or have been managing for many years, you have before you a compelling opportunity. Effectiveness, in greater measure than you have yet grasped, is now available. Effectiveness in management comes down to getting what you and your company need in a way that allows you to get it again and again.

It is done by the wise use of your influence.

There is a lie that must be named and a truth that must be told. The lie runs something like this, "You have to prepare for a profession, a craft or a job providing goods or services. It takes time and persistence to achieve excellence. But management comes naturally. If you were good on the front line and can think problems through in an organized way, experience will teach you how to manage well."

The truth that must be told is this. Management is a specialty. It has a body of knowledge, a group of skills and certain attitudes that support its practice. These can be learned, but the learning takes time and focused effort. It will involve training, study and perhaps finding a coach or mentor. Without such focused effort the learning curve is slow and the cost is high.

The president of a company that contracts with the state highway department to construct cement islands indicating turn lanes on highways told me: "I've got a problem. Where can I find management talent? I take my best guy who pours cement and make him the manager of a crew. I've lost my best pourer of cement, and he can't manage people!"

It is a challenge faced in every business, industry, not-for-profit organization and government agency—getting management talent. From pouring cement to managing the cardiology unit at a large research hospital, the best provider of goods or services will not, by virtue of those skills, make a great manager.

The problem is illustrated in the way the president of the company named it. Management talent is not found; it is developed. I asked him what he was doing to bring some of his employees to readiness to lead.

We have all known people who had ten years' experience on the job and others who have had one year of experience ten times. Experience is not the best teacher. Disciplined reflection on experience is. Reflection on practice leverages experience into knowledge. New choices for change, development and success become available to managers.

Experience is not the best teacher. Disciplined reflection on experience is.

To take yourself to greater effectiveness and efficiency in management, you need the leverage provided by career-long learning. There is no significant success without it. With it, managers empower themselves and their groups to achieve the one wildly important priority—results. They multiply their efforts, their influence and their effectiveness.

WHAT GOT YOU HERE

How did you come to be a manager? Looking into this is important. If you know who you are and how you got here, you will immediately have some clues where to go and how to get there.

It is no accident that you are in management. It didn't just happen. It has a lot to do with the kind of person you are—your aspirations, gifts, plans, hopes and values.

Much of that was established well before you were old enough to take your first job. Some of it came from what other people told you about yourself when you were very young. Maybe they saw something that was there before you had a name for it—leadership potential. Perhaps you believed them. Perhaps you were the oldest child in your family and expected to set an example for the younger ones. Perhaps your parents, because of their own struggles, needed you to be strong. You took others' view of you and made it a part of your self understanding.

Maybe experiences at school or in your neighborhood gave you a taste of leadership and you liked it.

Or maybe you didn't like others casting you in a certain mold and you began to listen more carefully to your own voice. In opposition, or even defiance, you shaped a strength that others didn't understand. Perhaps, even in this backhanded way, their voices had an influence, long forgotten, that helped bring you to leadership.

John Lennon, of Beatles fame, gave the aunt who raised him a gold plaque engraved with her oft-repeated advice to him when he was growing up: "You'll never make a living playing that guitar."

For whatever reasons, maybe you came to your potential to lead the slow way. You were young for your age and only awakened to your gifts later. Some late bloomers keep blooming longer.

The kind of person you are got you here and will be the single most powerful influence on your future in management.

If you're going to do the heavy lifting, as Archimedes suggested, you need "a place to stand on." We all stand on our own identity and history. The kind of person you are got you here and will be the single most powerful influence on your future in management.

There are some key attributes that influenced your path to management responsibility:

- *Mastery on the front line.* You probably became good at what you did on the front line, were dependable and were not too much of a pain in the assets of the company. Somebody saw all that and suspected you had management potential.

- *Ambition.* You want to achieve more. More than your peers. More than your parents. More than was expected of you. More in some other dimension. More. Ambition does not necessarily have a specific target. It is just an inner motivating force driving you toward achieving some more that you identify differently over time.

- *A wish to lead.* Early in life, when you got together with a group, there was something in you that wanted to lead. Before you even understood what it was, people saw it and asked you to be the captain, chair the committee or plan the party. Or maybe you came to this late. Maybe it was only after a few years in the world of work that you started to identify that there was something about being out front that appealed. Maybe somebody told you that if you're not the lead dog pulling the sled the view never changes. Maybe you felt you could do a better job than the leaders you saw.

- *A natural teacher.* You love passing along communal wisdom and knowledge. You have a sense of a lot of things that don't work and a few that do work in a company and enjoy helping others see what you see. Maybe you enjoy seeing others grow as their knowledge and reflection on experience take them to a new place. Maybe you love giving help, advice or support. Maybe you have a concern for excellence and contribution.

Some combination of these things, or a hundred others, brought you to personal readiness to move into management. Even if you made that move a number of years ago, don't forget those attributes. They are the foundation for your contribution. They will sustain you.

THE MOVE INTO MANAGEMENT

There is a cartoon that shows two men talking about their work and life. One of them says, "Then I made the leap from skilled labor to unskilled management."

Transitioning from operating to managing, a development process that does not coincide with promotion, may take a year or two or even longer. It is sometimes not well supported by companies. The move feels like a "leap" rather than a developmental journey. In this circumstance, a manager, avoiding the pleasure of casting blame, can take responsibility for his own learning and growth.

Without a self-chosen process of development, a manager will come to feel that she has crossed a border with a borrowed passport. There will be a lurking fear that says, "They are going to find me out—I am in over my head." This anxiety leads to all kinds of distancing from employees and a lack of authentic, helpful relationships with them.

Isaac Stern, one of the master violinists of the 20th century was interviewed once and asked what it was like for him to be a leader among musicians, to have even very good violinists come to him for coaching, to have so many people eager to attend his concerts. He said, "When you step out on that stage to play, and people have paid good money to hear you play, you had better know that you have earned the right to be there!"

Knowing that you have prepared, earned the right to be there, contributes to the quality of authentic presence that people follow. They experience you as "the real thing."

It is the same for leaders and managers in organizations. Knowing that you have prepared, earned the right to be there, contributes to the quality of authentic presence that people follow. They experience such a manager as "the real thing."

Managers, especially those new to the practice, confront a very personal question, "Do I want to be an authority for other people?"

I have asked thousands of people that question in the management development training I provide. Some answer with a clear and firm "Yes." But a great many reflect some ambivalence: "Well ... yes ... but ... "

Their ambivalence most often reflects mixed experiences with other authorities—those that have helped, those that have hurt, those that have shared their authority and those that have robbed others of the authority of their own thoughts, feelings and experiences.

Unease with authority costs a manager something. Employees can be heard saying things like, "I wish I could really know where she stands on this," or "He sometimes comes across like a dictator and other times seems so unsure. What is real here?"

If this is an issue for you, it may help to distinguish three modes of authority:

1. **Authority over.** Managers have authority over some things. Someone has to conduct the meeting. Someone has to sign off on the budget. Someone has to decide if new people can be hired this year. Someone has to conduct performance reviews. Authority over is given by the organization and is graphed on the organization chart.

   Managers are held responsible for having authority over some things. But if managers use that authority to talk down to people from a pedestal or coerce them, pretty soon their influence is diminished. Though the organization chart is a graphic representation of authority over, the real power to influence is given by followers. And they can take it away.

   Harry was puzzled. Most of the time he was making his numbers—getting the results his company expected of him. But it was getting harder than it had been his first year in management. And two of his best performers had left after letting it be known that their decision had something to do with his management style. As he saw the direction things were headed, he was anxious and felt the need to seek consultation about his career development.

   We reflected together on feedback from his manager, his direct reports and some of his peers. They had used a 360-degree feedback instrument in an effort to help Harry understand his effect on people and their patterns of response. Harry was able to see that some changes were in order if he was to ever realize his full potential. Highly motivated, Harry committed to work on developing two critical skills: 1) Listening and reflecting understanding and 2) Engaging in robust dialogue with his direct reports and giving serious consideration to their suggestions. A man of much potential, Harry was ready to grow.

2. **Authority with.** Authority with is given by other people. Everywhere I have ever worked, there were people who had no authority over me at all but whom I gave authority with me. It sounds like this, "When she talks, I better listen. She knows what she's talking about." As a manager, you want all of this you can get. But it is not something you can coerce. It is freely given. Or not.

Elizabeth had done so well in her first management job that she had recently been promoted to a position that would give greater scope to her talents. In the first two weeks, she saw many things that needed changing for greater efficiency of operation in her department. Thriving on the positive feelings from the promotion, she was inclined to make the changes that she was sure would get things moving.

I suggested, "Don't do it. Give your people time to come to trust you. Let them tell you what they see. Be present with them. You don't have to do everything you know how to do in your first month." We talked about how people come to give a manager authority to lead them. Elizabeth was on her way to a satisfying career.

3. **Authority for.** Authority for is something managers give themselves. The organization cannot grant it. The organization chart does not show it. Other people can't give it to you. You give it to yourself when you feel legitimate in doing so. Though every manager will communicate it differently, It sounds something like this: "I'm here for you. I've been down this road a lot, and it's my job to help you succeed. Let me know how I can help." You will know, and other people can tell, when your offer is genuine and reflects real readiness and comfort being in a position of authority.

Max felt unsure of himself for the first time in a long time. A hard driver, and a man of considerable accomplishments, his leadership style could be characterized as pacesetting. He led by example and personal heroics. When his direct reports were not performing up to speed on a project, Max would often jump in and make what he felt was a critical contribution that got the needed results. This style had led to successive promotions as a manager of successful units.

A position as a division director was opening up. When Max discussed the opportunity with the President of his company, she had told him that, while he was an excellent operations manager, she was not sure he would be comfortable in a role that placed him more distant from day-to-day operations. There, it would be his primary responsibility to help operations managers who might feel he was discounting their authority. Could he handle this? How would he use his experience and authority for their benefit? Max had a weekend of much reflection and not a little anxiety.

Responses to your authority will be as varied as you can imagine. Most employees you will lead will have some ambivalence about authority. This is no accident. They have had experience with authorities that helped them, hurt them, supported them, discounted them or encouraged them. These random experiences are the seedbed in which their current ambivalence flowers.

People with a lot of ambivalence will both want you to fix things for them and resist you when you try.

You need not interpret their dependence or their resistance as simply a response to your best efforts. It is also a lingering, and inappropriately continuing, response to all their past experience with authorities. It is not your responsibility to resolve their ambivalence. Just stay on course being trustworthy. Enough people will experience you as resourceful and supportive, and be ready to let you lead.

People who report to you will usually not ask it outright, but some will wonder, "By what authority do you presume to manage? Who do you think you are?" You need an answer you are comfortable with, even if they don't ask.

These questions certainly will be on the minds of your employees if you were at one time their peer. There will be occasions when you will need to open the discussion even if they don't. "Tom, we've been peers in this company for more than a year, even friends, and now I'm your manager. My hunch is that this will be a little awkward for me sometimes. What will it be like for you? We probably need to discuss this." You and Tom may need a ritual of transition something like this to forestall problems.

Who was the best manager you ever had? Think back. What was it about that person that made you willing to follow their leadership? What was it about them that got the group on board? How was it that they were so able to bring out the best contributions of people? Many things. But surely some of their gift was the ability to position themselves as an authority for you and others—willing to share their experience, strength and hope in ways that helped you understand your options.

Early in my career, a couple of years after graduate school, I was in an internship preparing for leadership and management. My supervisor during that year, Chuck Hall, asked me early on, "What do you want? What do you aspire to? Why are you here?" Being who I was, I told him that I wanted to sit in his chair—wanted to be the supervisor rather than the supervisee. He didn't throw me out. He let me know that would probably be possible, but that I would have to walk a road similar, but also very different, to the one he had walked—that getting there was a process rather than an event.

Becoming comfortable with your own authority for others often involves effecting some alliance with those who have been authorities for you. The alliance may be delayed and it may be known only to you. But there are still moments when I am in the role of manager and I do something that reminds me of what Chuck Hall would have done.

CHANGES IN IDENTITY, RESPONSIBILITY AND ROLE

As I was coaching a new manager one day, she said, "It's like last month I was complaining about how stupid management is, and this month I am management. It sure puts a different light on things!" The view changes when you become a manager. Where you stand on things depends on where you sit. Establishing new identity, taking up new responsibilities, getting comfortable in the new role—these processes evolve over time. Getting hired or promoted is just the start.

There is loss as well as gain when you move into management. You loose the freedom to play "Ain't it awful" with the people on the front line. There is a certain pleasure in playing that game, but managers must give it up. Great managers manage their own feelings and model the attitudes they want to inspire in their followers.

When you move into management, you no longer are "one of the guys" or "one of the gals." Managers uneasy being an authority for people may try to side-step this reality. But your direct reports understand it. They know that a manager has organizational power in a measure that they do not.

There will be times when their knowledge will be to your benefit. On those occasions when push comes to shove, you may say to an employee, "Because I am responsible for this unit in a way that you are not, I'm going to have to make this decision. I hope you can get on board."

The move into management signals the formation of a new identity. Management is not only something you do—a practice. It also becomes who you are. This is not about ego expansion. It is about what your company needs from you. It is about what the people you lead need from you. It is about positioning yourself to have the influence you will need in order to get the results you and your company need. Positioned as a "buddy," you will get compliance (if you are lucky); you will not get excellence.

The call to excellence, the call to stretch beyond present capacity, does not usually come from a peer. Think back. Who supported you with the confrontation that you could do better than you were doing? Who told you that you were capable of more than you had achieved? Who told you that if you were going to get what you wanted you would have to ask for it more clearly? Who identified a strength that you had not yet claimed? Who said that if you really applied yourself you could excel? Most of those voices, calling you to your full potential, were probably not the voices peers.

To excel in management, you will need to issue such calls and convey that you expect people to hear and respond. Managers issue such calls through their words and their attitudes as they model the changes they want to see.

Managers at most levels find ways to demonstrate that they can cut it on the front line. This draws respect for both your willingness and your skill. One day I said to the man helping me carry groceries to my car, "I thought you were the manager here." He replied, "I am, but I've learned that it's a lot easier to pull than it is to push."

Balancing this willingness to demonstrate operational competence, managers guard against being seduced back into too much involvement in providing the product or service. Managers are paid to manage, not to operate.

Gravitating back to operations work is, for some managers, a retreat to a former comfort zone. We all dance the dance we know best. Some managers find evolution into the new identity particularly stressful until their skills, attitudes and practices catch up with their new responsibilities.

It's a matter of balance. No one can tell you what the proper balance is. You will set your own balance based on your growth as a manager, your sense of what your team needs this week, your sensitivity to their response to you and the urgency of the results you are responsible to produce.

Another manager I was coaching had been transferred to a department that had a history of trouble. He started with high energy and great hope. One day a couple of months later he said, "I don't know what to do. This is driving me to distraction. Every time I try to launch a new initiative my people protest that top leadership (not me!) is messing things up again." I asked, "Exactly how do they put it?" He said, "They say, 'They … they … they. They're doing it to us again.' "

I suggested that the problem was positioning. He was letting people position him as the "good guy" and top leadership as the "bad guy." I asked, "What would it be like, next time that happens, to say to them that you are they … that there is no absent villain—that you are responsible for executing this challenging change that you and the rest of the management team have committed to, that you know they are the kind of people who can get it done, that you are there to help them get it done—and ask them to talk with you about how best to get it done?"

He lit up like a five-year-old on Christmas morning. He said, "I can do this." A month later it was evident that he was beginning to turn the department around.

Middle managers represent top leadership to the front line and represent the front line to top leadership. Their power to influence the front line comes from positioning themselves to speak for the needs of the company. Positioning yourself as the "good guy" in contrast with other "bad guys" never works. You lose respect and credibility.

The new role and responsibility will at times require that you speak from your confidence, not from your doubts and misgivings. Even when you don't agree a hundred and ten percent with a decision of the management team you are part of, it is your responsibility to represent the decision to front-line employees and bring them along. You properly express your disagreement and suggestions for new directions to your manager—not to your direct reports.

Great managers ask their groups to trust that they know where they are going, that they know the direction ahead, even when what they really see is only the next couple of turns in the road. Because they have the wider view that management provides, they are very aware of the ifs, ands and buts. They know, and feel, the pitfalls that may lie ahead, that there are many contingencies that cannot be accurately predicted. But they ask people to trust them and move ahead. People need the leader's confidence. They have enough doubts of their own.

FROM DEVELOPING YOURSELF TO DEVELOPING OTHERS

Before you became a manager, your focus was on developing yourself—your knowledge base, your skills, your ability to work as a member of a productive team and your interpersonal skills. As a manager, your focus is on developing others.

A manager who doesn't respond to this shift in focus tends to attract and keep people who want to hold a job, not expand their capacity and make themselves more valuable in the workplace. The result is a team that coasts and doesn't produce the results that are needed.

> If you want to keep your best employees until they're are ready either for promotion or to move on, be a career builder.

Most of the people who report to you will leave your employ. This is not your grandfather's world of work. It is rare for people to spend their working life in one company and retire. The people you will want on your team are people who want to leave your employ better prepared than when they came. They will want to know that what they are doing, and your leadership contributes not just to the company, but to their personal future. If you want to keep your best employees until they are ready either for promotion or to move on, be a career builder.

Some managers fear that this causes them to lose good people. Yes, but it will attract more good people than you will lose. There is no better way to attract able and ambitious people to your unit than having the reputation of a career builder.

WHAT GOT YOU HERE WON'T GET YOU WHERE YOU CAN GO

Whether you're a first-time manager or have been in management for many years, here is an insight into your future—what got you to this level won't enable you to become all that you can be or to achieve all that you can achieve.

Everyone is a highly individual blend of energy, knowledge, aspiration, skills, insight, wisdom, drive, ambition, understandings, values, ideals and human-relations abilities. The blend that defines your uniqueness is what brought you to where you are today.

> Listen to the voice within you. Know what you really want and don't want, what you are fit for and what you are not fit for. Your ability to lead and manage rests on who you truly are and what you truly want.

Lawrence J. Peter published a book in 1968, *The Peter Principle*, in which he stated that people tend, over time and through promotions, to rise to their level of incompetence. His title became an oft-repeated humorous explanation by employees of what they regarded as the deficiencies of their boss. While there is some truth here about organizational life, what the Peter Principle misses is that people have a drive toward what psychologist Abraham Maslow called "self actualization." Staying at the level of present capacity (or incapacity) is not satisfying once a person makes a felt connection between their underdeveloped gifts and what is possible.

This is not about chronic dissatisfaction and agitation to move up the organization chart clawing and scratching your way to the top. It truly is about self actualization—developing and using all the gifts that are in you. Career-long development and self-actualization can be nurtured at any organizational level.

Maslow was the first born of seven children born to uneducated immigrants. Eager to see their oldest son succeed in the new world, they pushed him hard for academic success. To satisfy them, he began the study of law. But it didn't satisfy him. It was not what his life was about. It didn't resonate with who he was. And he knew it.

Relatively late, he became interested in psychology and found that it was what he was about. He knew that, for him, psychology was not just an academic discipline. It spoke to who he was. It allowed him to manifest an essential part of his being. If he had not discovered that, think of the torments of the unfulfilled that he would have suffered.

A few years after his death, Maslow's insights became the basis of the most expansive recruiting campaign ever used by the US military, the Army's "Be all you can be" campaign. Listen to the voice within you. Know what you really want or don't want, what you are fit for and what you are not fit for. Your ability to lead and manage rests on who you truly are and what you truly want.

Your personal capacities were the strongest influence in getting you into management. What will take you to the next level of effectiveness has a lot more to do with your thoughts, beliefs and feelings about other people's capacities.

Some things last. After the new thing in management (MBO, TQM, strategic planning, change management, the balanced scorecard, execution, etc.) has disappeared and even the new new thing is about to fade, some of the foundational work of the fathers and mothers of modern management theory remains.

In 1957, Douglas McGregor showed the practical application of Maslow's psychology to the world of work. He described two models of understanding people at work which he called Theory X and Theory Y. His book, *The Human Side of Enterprise*, published in 1960, helps managers understand how their view of human nature, particularly human nature at work, becomes a powerful influence on the contribution employees make to a company.

Theory X says:

- People don't like work and will avoid it if they can

- People don't want responsibility and would rather have someone else direct them

- People must be controlled, forced or threatened with consequences if they are going to achieve organizational objectives

- Therefore, management's role is to direct, coerce and control employees

Few managers would say that they hold these beliefs. But scratch deeper and you can see that the command and control and micromanagement styles are the natural offspring of these core beliefs. Despite protestations to the contrary, these styles have not been laid to rest.

Theory Y says:

- Work is as natural to human nature as play and rest

- People will direct themselves to constructive work if they are committed to worthy objectives

- They will be committed to objectives if there are rewards for achieving them

- People learn to accept and seek responsibility

- Imagination, ingenuity and creativity are widely distributed among the population. People are capable of using these qualities to solve organizational problems

- People have potential

Someone once said, "That's OK in practice, but how does it work out in theory?" Few things are so practical as a good theory. Managers whose core beliefs are closer to Theory Y see their opportunity to develop the potential of employees and help them use that potential to achieve shared goals. Managers whose core beliefs lead to practices that reflect Theory X will be locked into feelings of powerlessness and complain that the workforce is not full of more willing people.

SET YOUR COURSE FOR SELF DEVELOPMENT

What do you want out of your work? Really want? When you get clear about that, you are ready to grow yourself beyond what got you where you are today.

The prospect of becoming all that you can be, developing your capacity to influence others to be all that they can be, will begin to have a powerful attraction. Your full capacity will not necessarily unfold with the passage of time. But you can set a course for yourself. You are going where you feel you have the right to be. You are going where your learning will take you.

Action Steps You Can Take

To leverage your personal qualities for more influential management, reflect on these points and make some notes.

- What were the formative experiences in your life before the age of eighteen that may have a lot to do with you winding up in management?

- What do you know about yourself (your personality, style and ways of relating) that contributes to your value as a manager?

- What do you know about yourself that could get in the way of using your best knowledge and skills?

- What are your strongest beliefs about people at work?

- Read *The 7 Habits of Highly Effective People* by Stephen R. Covey. Identify which of the habits come naturally for you and which are ones you want to develop.

- How could use of a 360-degree feedback instrument be helpful? Do you want to consider using one?

- Write down a few goals for developing your influence as a manager over the next year. Write how you will pursue those goals.

The 2nd Lever: Self Management

Managing others is not the foundation. Managing yourself is. This foundation will support, or undermine, everything else you do. Brilliant and well-intentioned managers have seen their effectiveness drowned in a tsunami of inadequate self-management. Less brilliant managers have excelled because they built this foundation well.

YOUR WILDLY
IMPORTANT PRIORITIES

Every manager has hundreds of things that could command attention every day. No manager has enough time and energy to respond to all of them. As one manager said, "It's like the blanket is never big enough for the bed. Just about the time you pull some cover over this way, somebody over there gets cold." It's one of the basic problems of management. The multiple events that press forward every day do not by themselves give a manager any clue which is meaningful and which is merely distracting background noise.

It has become trite to say that you must prioritize. It's said so much that people hastily agree and then proceed without prioritizing. Don't be too hasty. Prioritizing requires reflection and decision making—one of the core practices of management. That takes time. Under the influence of urgency addiction, managers come to feel that they don't have the time to invest in reflection. Action sidelines prioritizing.

> Great managers reframe the principle of prioritization in a way that makes the practice compelling. Prioritizing becomes, for them, a practice rather than a fine principle that someone else ought to use.

Prioritization got reframed for me one day in the Atlanta airport when I was traveling to speak somewhere in the Midwest. I noticed that the officers of the Transportation Security Administration (TSA) were all dressed in their uniforms and looked nice. They didn't look like they had just come off a ten-day camping trip in the mountains of Northeast Georgia where I live. It occurred to me that some manager must have told them, "That's a priority. Look professional."

When I went through the gate they detected a small pocket knife that I had neglected to put in my suitcase. They took my picket knife, but they were nice to me. Even though I had violated the prescribed procedure, they didn't treat me like a criminal. It was cold comfort, but they even smiled as they took away my knife. It occurred to me that some manager must have told them, "That's a priority. Be nice to the customers." It is a Wildly Important Priority for them.

You can use this concept, and the acronym WIP, to help you move prioritization from the realm of "good ideas" into disciplined execution. I called the Performance Improvement Director of a large hospital a year after I had provided a retreat for their senior management group. She said, "Interesting you called today. In our meeting yesterday, we were identifying our WIPs for the new year." Here is a rare thing—an idea that turns a familiar concept (prioritizing) into a usable tool.

Don't call it prioritizing. Call it identifying your WIPs. Words really do make a difference.

Great managers know that the main thing is to keep the main thing the main thing.

Human nature isn't wired to handle sixteen priorities. Three, four, maybe five on your best week, or month, or quarter, or year. Great managers identify just a few and nail them to the wall of their consciousness. Then, by skillful and repeated communication, they hold them in sharp focus in front of the team they lead.

MANAGING YOUR COMMUNICATION

Skillful communication is a large order. A number of research studies of management communication have shown that in most companies, most employees feel that their managers have not made clear what the priorities are, what they are supposed to do to act on the priorities or how performance rewards (money and promotions) align with execution on the priorities.

Most managers are shocked to hear this. "I told them! Goodness knows how many times I've told them. They're not stupid people. How can they not know?"

Telling is not the same thing as communicating. How many times do parents tell their children to do something that is important, but come to realize that it has not become important to the children?

There is a half-truth that will help you here. You might want to write it on your soul if not on your desk. "It is my responsibility to persuade, not theirs to agree." Yes, it is only a half truth, but living by it will sharpen your thinking about your communication.

Boyd Clarke and Ron Crossland, writing in *The Leader's Voice*, say, "The biggest problem with leadership communication is the illusion that it has occurred." Their insight into this challenge is penetrating. Leaders, they say, make four fatal assumptions about how employees receive their communication. They assume that employees:

1. Understand

2. Agree

3. Care

4. Will take appropriate action

Managers who want their telling to turn into communication test these assumptions in robust dialogue. Robust dialogue is a concept of great usefulness for managers. It engages people to draw out their response to your telling them what you want to tell them:

- Do they agree?

- Do they see something that you may have overlooked?

- Do they disagree?

- Do they think it is a good idea, but that the timing may not be right?

- Does it really matter?

- What difference do they think your idea could make?

- Would it make things better or worse?

- What actions do they think would be needed to put legs under the idea?

- Do they really feel ready to go?

- What might they need, that they don't have now, in order to feel ready to go?

- What's first?

- When should the initiative be launched? By whom? How?

> Great managers look carefully to see if they have managed their communication well before assuming that their job is to manage the resistance of employees.

Persuasive communication is brief, memorable and repeated often. Millions are spent to show the same thirty-second commercial on television hundreds of times until it sticks with us. "Where's the beef?" "I'm loving it." "The pause that refreshes." Great managers learn to say the same thing in twenty different ways so that the repetition is not irritating.

Managers have read much, thought much, discussed much and even taken training on getting "buy-in" from employees. Buy-in is not enough. It is a metaphor from finance. It carries the attitude, "If the reward is significant enough and if the price is right, I will buy in." It says that a bargain has been struck between the manager and a subordinate. Such a bargain will get compliance. It will not produce exceptional performance.

Managers want more than employees who will buy into their objectives. Managers need employees who carry the mind-set of owners, not customers who have bought what the manager is selling. It is the miracle of dialogue that takes associates to the entrepreneurial attitude of an owner. Giving thoughtful consideration to your communication, you can invite expression of the values and objectives of employees and show common ground with the values and objectives of the company and your unit. By doing this, you enlist people. They will bring their passion and energy to work.

There is an often-repeated story from the oral history of American business that might even be true. It goes that Steve Jobs, the founder of Apple Computer went one day to try to recruit the President of Pepsi Cola to leave his job and come to work for Apple. Supposedly, after a walk they went up one of the giant buildings that marks the New York City skyline. Looking out over the metropolis Steve Jobs asked, "Do you want to sell sugar water the rest of your life? Or do you want to change the world?"

The point of the story is not that soft drinks are bad and computers are good. There are times when only a Pepsi or Coke will do. And many have experienced that there are times when they want to throw the computer over a cliff. The point is this—Steve Jobs knew his man. He knew communication—how to communicate with words that would powerfully resonate with the values and aspirations of another.

How about you? Do you want to change the world? Or maybe at least change the room you are in? You can. Find your authentic voice. Speak from your convictions. Listen to the voice, aspirations and convictions of the people you lead. Find the magic point where your and their intentions converge. Communicate!

MANAGING YOUR TIME

Ask ten managers what their three steepest challenges are—you will probably hear a lot about time stress. It's built into the reality of managing and organizational life that a considerable amount of a manager's time must be spent on concerns that do not produce the contribution to results that a manager needs.

- Resolving today's problems created by last year's solution distracts from a proper focus on next year's opportunities

- Internal events pull attention away from those changing trends outside the organization that become so risky to the viability of the organization if they are neglected

- Today's crisis drains energy needed for reflection and decision making on readjusting priorities and ways to address them

- Intervening with nonperforming employees distracts from developing future star performers

- Operating leaves insufficient time for managing

These are not problems to be solved. They are the turf on which managers operate. These things must be done. The pathway to effective contribution does not lie in agitated resistance to these necessities or fantasizing about a more ideal reality. The pathway to effectiveness lies instead in rigorous use of three practices:

1. Take a careful look at your use of time by keeping a log for a week or two in which you keep record of how you use your time. See how much of your time is really spent in the activities described in the bullets above—most managers will find that up to eighty percent of their working time is spent there. How much of your time is unaccounted for due to relating and socializing? (Yes, some of this is valuable.)

2. Examine your involvement in the five major time wasters to see how you could improve the investment of your time:

   a. Disconnected Wildly Important Priorities (WIPs)
   b. Perfectionism
   c. A disorganized work area
   d. Allowing excessive interruptions
   e. Ineffective meetings

3. Concentrate the time not accounted for in practice number one and the time saved in practice number two into major blocks of time committed to high-priority, results-producing work. Many managers feel that an uninterrupted hour and a half is a minimum for significant work on those things that build effectiveness.

These practices take managers out of feeling victimized by events and put them in control of their time. This is empowering. Daily events or your decisions will determine how you spend your time. Letting events control is a formula for ineffectiveness. Time management is about self management.

See if any of the five major time wasters make your daily time pressures more challenging than they would otherwise be:

- **Disconnected Wildly Important Priorities (WIPs).** This is different than unclear goals and priorities. Managers generally know what the their priorities are. But if you have a fuzzy sense of how those priorities are going to steer your work this week, the priorities get disconnected from reality, and the door to time stress if flung wide open. Reconnecting requires not only saying "yes" to the WIP, but also saying "no" to those activities that don't contribute to results. Effective managers focus on results, not activities.

  Many managers keep a "To Do" list. This often causes more stress than it resolves, particularly if you start each day with a long list for that day that doesn't reflect prioritization and hard choices. Reality intrudes, and the day ends in discouragement.

  It is better to just identify a few Wildly Important Priorities for the week and retain some flexibility in how you invest your time on a daily basis. That way you don't finish the day defeated because you didn't accomplish the sixty-seven things on your to do list. Also, you keep yourself on track with what is most important. You will find that saying "Yes" to the few WIPs and keeping them at the forefront of your attention makes it possible to say "No" to less important things.

- **Perfectionism.** Perfectionist strivings paralyze constructive action. The good is sacrificed in the name of the perfect. When you feel stuck because you don't have all the information you need in order to make a decision, remind yourself that many times second best in operation is better than first best on the drawing board. Most management decisions must be made without 100% of the information that could be useful. Organizations are too complex for a manager to know everything.

Most great managers have a bent toward action. They do not get trapped in reflection. After due consideration (not too much) they come to the wisdom of the slogan of Nike, Inc.—"Just Do It." A great manager told me once that his attitude was "Do something; you can apologize tomorrow."

- **A disorganized work area.** What does your desk look like? What do your files look like? Managers can't afford to waste time looking for things in the clutter.

  There are some things you could do …

  1. Form the habit of clearing your desk top before finishing work each day. This is not just advice from you mother who likes to keep things tidy. It will leave you with a sense of having completed the day's work. It will let you face the next morning with a sense of having a fresh start. It will keep things filed so that you will not have to rummage through stacks of files and bits of paper to find something.

  2. Follow the much repeated advice "Handle each piece of paper that comes to your desk only once." It is amazing how this practice will keep your work space, and your mind, safe from attacks by the clutter monster. Avoid any temptation to tell yourself, "I'll handle that later." Just do it!: File it, act on it or trash it. Most people keep too much. When you receive a memo, you could hand write your response on it and send it right back to the author.

  3. Use a "Current Projects" file. Keep it close by where you can retrieve it without having to look for it. Use it to file the things you are currently working on that can't be finished in a day or week—things that need to stay on your front burner.

  4. Stop writing on loose papers. They pile up and are hard to find later. Use a spiral-bound notebook. Date each page and enter all your notes on phone calls, requests from colleagues and brilliant ideas to follow up on later.

- **Allowing excessive interruptions.** People will waste your time. Great managers decide how to use their time. They structure their availability to others. Of course they are available for unplanned discussions of operating problems that are both urgent and important. But if a manager is always responsive to other people's definition of what is urgent and important, dependency is fostered, and the manager is drained and distracted from making his best contribution.

There are four things you can do.

1. Protect blocks of time for work that is important but not urgent: planning, evaluating, coaching conferences with individuals, etc. Sometimes you will need ninety minutes of uninterrupted time. Let it be known that you are not available, except for emergencies, when your door is closed. Designate an hour or two a day for "open door."

2. Be available in other people's work space. Walk around when you decide to be available. It is easier to leave than to get people to leave your space.

3. Manage telephone and E-mail availability. Bunch them together and have a designated time to return messages each day. To get off the phone, use the closing gambit (one meaning of "gambit" in the dictionary is a remark used to open or redirect a conversation), "Before we hang up, I need to make one quick point … "

4. When an unplanned visitor comes in, stand up. Don't offer them a chair unless you decide the discussion must take place immediately. Don't make a lot of small talk. Ask what they need and how you can help. Then either decide to immediately discuss the issue or make an appointment for later in the day or week. Use the closing gambit, "One more quick thing before you go … " Walk toward the door.

- **Ineffective meetings.** Peter Drucker, whom many say wrote the "Bible" on management, was Professor of Management at New York University for over twenty years. *The New York Times*, in his obituary, quoted him as having said, "One either meets or one works." Most of the time people in meetings plan work or report on work in progress. Most productivity comes outside of meetings.

Whenever you can, avoid meeting just because it is time for the regular meeting. If there is nothing that needs action by the group, don't meet. Launch meetings with a concise statement of why you are meeting and the important things that the group needs to decide or act on. This will cause people to come to meetings feeling that something important is going to happen.

Since they are necessary, effective managers use some of these six ways of making the best use of meetings:

1. Start and end on time. This becomes a powerful symbolic communication: that the meeting is important, that you respect the time of those attending and that they can expect that the next meeting will also start on time. Acknowledge late comers by name and without a warm smile. End the meeting on a positive note.

2. After fifty minutes, have people stand up for the rest of the meeting. It results in a lot less chatter. The first time I heard this recommendation, I thought it funny but didn't know if I had the nerve to try it. Try it. You'll like it. People will get the message and some will even get the humor.

3. Circulate an agenda in advance that lists topics to be discussed, time limits for each, and decisions to be made.

4. Prep people for their contributions—how long they will have to introduce an issue and what you need to have covered. You can even "stack the deck" by letting an individual know that you would appreciate them voicing what you know to be their perspective in the course of a given discussion.

5. Conduct the meeting. Like a conductor of an orchestra you establish the focus, move the action along, foreclose verbosity and the telling of stories, press for decisions and commitments to action.

6. Ask the person who takes minutes to write brief summaries of discussion and to include a paragraph headed by the word "Action" that documents decisions made on each agenda item and who is responsible. This makes it easy for people to review the minutes when they are circulated. It also begins to form your agenda for the next meeting.

MANAGING YOUR ANXIETIES

Management is difficult. Managers are held responsible for the outcome of actions and events over which they have no direct influence. No manager can know whether everything their direct reports are doing is wise or will contribute to desired outcomes. Influence is often indirect—a function of management practices like inspiring, modeling, clarifying priorities and coaching. At times a manager has little control over whether, or when, these practices will lead to effective execution.

Also, there is always a multitude of facts and forces at work in an organization. No manager can hold all of these in consciousness all the time and always make wise decisions.

Systems in affluent developed countries evolve toward greater and greater complexity. Influences multiply. Cause and effect are often less than crystal clear. Human error cannot be eradicated. Anticipating the future is a chancy business. It's one of the perils of a career in management that managers are held responsible for outcomes over which they have imperfect control.

The minutiae of day-to-day challenges can obsess most managers and too narrowly focus their vision and attention. The result is inattention to the results—which are always external to the organization. Great managers resist this powerful drift and ask themselves, "What is the outcome, the total effect of all our internal activities, on the external realities that determine our success or failure?"

President Harry S. Truman had a gift for colorful language. His most memorable quote was, "If you can't stand the heat, get out of the kitchen." Another was on an engraved plaque on his desk in the oval office, "The buck stops here."

Managers, even those in the oval office, live in the anxious knowledge that the buck stops with them. Make your peace with it. Successful managers avoid excuse-making at every opportunity. People discount managers who blame him, her or it.

If this anxious knowledge, the heat, the uncertainty and the broad scope are not managed well, and if a manager has an exaggerated need for control, two undesirable outcomes are likely:

1. Anxiety takes a personal toll that becomes disabling

2. The anxiety spawns the practice of micromanagement that reduces the operational effectiveness and efficiency of employees

Who is taking care of the manager while the manager is busy taking care? Self care is a foundational mandate for every manager.

Stress is unavoidable for managers. The work is important and demanding. The risks are real. Managing the unavoidable stress well keeps it from evolving into avoidable distress.

Give these questions some quiet reflection:

- On a scale of 1 – 10 (10 being the most stressful), what is my stress level now?
- How adequate are the measures I now take for stress management?
- Who is responsible for burnout? Someone else, or me?
- What can/will I do for better self care?

Familiar measures are easy to list:

- Exercise
- Protecting time for family
- Occasional long weekends and an annual vacation
- Limiting taking work home
- A contemplative corner of your own—a place and time to reflect, ponder and call your soul your own
- Having a friend in whom you can confide
- An occasional reward for an accomplishment
- Play
- An avocation unrelated to your career
- Meditation or other spiritual practices
- Having a mentor in management (not your boss)

Listing is easy. Choices often are not. The ability to manage your stress is not a fixed quality, forever limited by your personality and established once and for all time. In a blinding flash of the obvious, a patient in a counseling group for substance abuse once said, "You know, if we don't change direction, we're going to wind up where we're headed!" Even when powerful forces have set a pattern for you, choices can be made.

CORE BELIEFS

A manager's stress arises as much from her core beliefs as from company-wide challenges and the high-maintenance people on her team. Her core beliefs have a profound effect on the stress level, and consequent effectiveness, of team members. This insight is beautifully developed by *Leading From Within* author Parker J. Palmer in a chapter describing what he calls the "shadow side of leaders."

Take a close look at the possibility that negative core beliefs are compromising your effectiveness and the efficiency of your group. Negative core beliefs are not inconsequential and harmless ideas. They set powerful processes in motion. They lead to dysfunctional management practices.

Here are some core beliefs to watch out for:

1. "If they see any imperfections in me, I will lose authority." For some managers, the drive for leadership has come at the cost of great effort to achieve personal mastery over their own felt deficiencies. This is the seedbed of the anxiety reflected in this core belief. It is the concern that what has been resolved in the past may come undone.

   While these dynamics are understandable, great managers know that the mask of perfection yields mistrust of a manager. Conversely, when associates see that a manager admits failure of well intentioned effort and learns from the failure, they sense that they are being led by an authentic person. Authenticity breeds trust.

2. "Unless I keep everything under control, things will fall apart. If anything valuable is to happen here I must do it myself or manage it closely." The first core belief reflects mistrust of self; this one reflects mistrust of others. The problem with this belief is that it becomes a self-fulfilling prophecy. Believing this, managers act in ways that bring it to pass. By managing so tightly, they rob associates of the opportunity to make their best contribution. They see the belief as reflecting reality without knowing that they help create the reality. They are like the person who fears that their marriage partner will leave them and therefore controls them to the point that they do leave.

Great managers operate out of a different core belief. They understand that given clear direction for a task that is worthy of their best, people will exercise initiative. Great managers manage the motivational environment by trusting associates. They start by giving trust rather than waiting for it to be earned.

3. "Life is a battleground of winners and losers. If somebody else wins, I lose." This belief rests on a misunderstanding of the way the world works. It assumes that life is a zero-sum game. More there means less here. In reality, more there makes it possible to work together so that there is more here, too. Even competition contributes to the performance of both competitors. A good deal is a good deal for everybody, or the deal won't last.

In the grip of this negative core belief, managers will inappropriately take credit for an associate's performance and cast blame on the associate for the manager's failures in performance. This behavior is not hard to spot. A manager's subordinates, peers and superiors will identify it. The manager loses credibility.

MANAGING YOUR STYLE

Pogo, a possum in the Okefenokee Swamp of Georgia, was created by Walt Kelly for a comic strip that ran for over twenty-five years. Pogo spoke in one strip about the pollution and trash that people brought to the swamp. He said, in what is probably the most oft quoted line from any comic strip in history, "We have met the enemy and he is us." The line can be taken as a reminder to managers that the most powerful barriers to effectiveness are often self-imposed.

What is your answer to this multiple choice question? Most managers who fail do so because:

    ___ They aren't smart enough

    ___ They haven't been to enough training workshops

    ___ They don't have the core skills of management

    ___ Their style of engaging others causes people to move away from them and against them rather than toward them and with them

Almost everyone I have asked this question checks the last answer. People skills trump technical skills. Every time. Almost any manager will find some people who respond positively to his or her characteristic and predominant style. Problems arise when managers have a "one style fits all" approach to using their predominant style.

There has been much discussion and writing about managerial style. The bottom line is this—there is no one correct style of management.

Among the managers who reported to me in a leadership position I held, there were two whose styles differed widely. William was as gentle and accommodating as you can imagine. Jack, who in his former career had been a Drill Sergeant, was a tough hell-raiser who took no prisoners. Both were very effective. The secret was this. William could be tough and Jack could be gentle. They were not captives of their predominant style. People gladly followed both.

Great managers know their predominant style, but employ it flexibly and borrow from other styles depending on the situation, the need and the people involved. Rigid application of one style to all circumstances is a recipe for failure.

If your only tool is a hammer, all your problems are going to look like nails. The challenge is to manage your styles rather than letting one style manage you.

> Most managers can tell you what their predominant style is. For greatness, they must understand it, use it flexibly and expand it by the use of additional styles.

The June 2006 issue of the *Harvard Business Review* carried an article titled "Leadership Run Amok—The Destructive Potential of Overachievers," in which they identified six styles used by managers to lead others:

- Directive
- Visionary
- Affiliative
- Participative
- Pacesetting
- Coaching

The styles are described as having their foundation in the motives driving a manager in any style or situation:

- Achievement
- Affiliation
- Power (Personalized Power and Socialized Power)

Self-knowledge is not just a nice idea. It saves a manager from the high cost of self-delusion. Unexamined styles and motives yield rigidity and inflexibility. These traits cause a manager to apply a familiar repertoire of interventions to all situations and individuals. Self-knowledge opens the door for expanding your range of competence in a greater variety of circumstances. Most managers I coach find that expanding self-awareness is a launching pad for greater success and personal satisfaction.

The first path to self-knowledge is reflection and rigorous honesty. It is hard for a busy manager to make time for reflection. Managers are inclined toward action more than reflection. At the extreme, this can look like urgency addiction. Some managers become anxious when the action stops. Vacations become harder to take. Personal and family time become squeezed. Even the need for rest and sleep are neglected.

You can get some sense of your style and motivating drive by reflecting on a few questions:

- **Motivating drive.** What do you like best? What energizes you?

  —Making a difference through a significant accomplishment (Achievement)?

  —Building working relationships that contribute to better business outcomes (Affiliation)?

  —Being seen as strong, important, the "go to guy or gal" (Personalized Power)?

  —Helping individuals and groups develop their capacities, feel capable and make a stronger contribution (Socialized Power)?

  Perhaps you enjoy all of these activities in some measure. Try to rank them in order of the satisfaction they provide you.

- **Styles.** What do you find yourself doing most of the time when you are working with your direct reports?

  —Giving directions about what to do, when and how. Bringing consequences (both positive and negative) to bear based on the performance of subordinates. Establishing the objective and then making sure that people execute on it. (Directive Style).

  —Showing a clear connection between the preferred and possible future of the organization, department or team and immediate responsibilities and challenges. Putting legs under strategy. Communicating with great clarity. (Visionary Style).

  —Being highly responsive to individual team members and their needs. Valuing people over task. Trying to build team cohesion by avoiding conflict. (Affiliative Style).

  —Encouraging people to participate in decision-making. Valuing collaboration over direction. Supporting people to make their voice heard. (Participative Style).

  —Leading by example. Jumping from management work into operations work when it looks like a group may not achieve an excellent outcome from their efforts. Enjoying being the model. (Pacesetting Style).

  —Mentoring people. Giving high priority to the development of direct reports, building their skills. (Coaching Style)

  You may have elements of all of the styles but probably can identify the one or two that you rely on most often. All are useful in certain situations and with certain people.

Great managers develop an intuitive sense of what is needed. Call it situational awareness. Karl Albrecht writes:

> The "S" Factor in the … model represents your Situational Awareness, a.k.a. your situational "radar." Are you able to understand and empathize with people in different situations? Can you sense their feelings and possible intentions? How well do you "read" situations based on a practical knowledge of human nature? Situational Awareness includes a knowledge of the cultural "holograms"—the unspoken background patterns, paradigms, and social rules that govern various situations. It means having an appreciation for the various points of view others might hold, and practical sense of the ways people react to stress, conflict, and uncertainty.

Managers ask themselves:

- "What is needed today that would have been less than helpful yesterday?"
- "Is it time to become more directive with Jack since his performance is slipping?"
- "Sam is going through a painful personal loss. Is it time to cut him some slack?"
- "Mary could handle situations like that much better; is it time for me to spend some time coaching her?"
- "The group seems to be in more conflict recently; is it time for me to call them to the overarching goal and the need to understand and resolve the conflict?"
- "The group looks down this morning. What is it about? How can I best respond in the meeting this afternoon?"

With experience, this kind of thinking and deciding among styles becomes more intuitive, more fluid and happens more often.

> Great managers develop an intuitive sense of what is needed and draw on a different style of engagement today than yesterday, a different style with Sue than with Joan, a different style in high-stress and low-stress situations.

Difficulties arise when a manager encounters a **cross-grained experience**—an experience in which what seems to be needed goes against the grain of the personality of the manager.

- Bob must be confronted about inadequate performance, but his manager doesn't confront him because he gets very uncomfortable in conflictual situations.

- Lois has done an excellent job completing a major project on time and under budget, but her manager doesn't praise her because she is uncomfortable giving praise.

- Carl needs to learn to assert his own ideas more clearly and strongly, but his manager doesn't talk with him about it because he feels that it is inappropriate to discuss an employee's personal issues.

Such cross-grained experiences usually are in a manager's blind spot. She doesn't see what would have been helpful since seeing it would have provoked anxiety. If the manager has a coach who asks, "I wonder why you didn't consider taking more direct action?" the manager may answer something like, "It just didn't occur to me."

A second path to self-knowledge is **feedback from colleagues**—peers, direct reports and superiors. You are lucky if you have a few people who will tell you who you are. If their insight is not forthcoming, find the courage to ask one or two whom you trust. When they give it, don't offer explanations or rebuttal. Simply thank them and say that you will reflect on what they have given you.

A lot of management research shows that when a manager asks for suggestions for improvements, chooses a couple of objectives and works on them for a few months, noticeable improvements are made.

A third path to self-knowledge is simply to **try something new and see if it fits** better than you anticipated that it would. For a month, commit yourself to looking for situations where an identified style that does not come naturally to you could appropriately be tried. Try it. When you receive feedback that sounds on-target, decide to use it and change your behavior for a week. You may find that the positive results outweigh the initial negative feelings that always accompany change.

Self management is clearly the foundation of all success as a manager. Developing and managing your ability to influence and persuade, clarifying and managing your priorities, becoming a great communicator, making the best use of your time, resolving your anxieties, and expanding your style—these things make everything else possible. Everything.

Self management is a lever of enormous power. Get a good grip!

Action Steps You Can Take

Here are some steps you could take that will leverage your self-management up a level.

- The last thing each week, write down your three to five Wildly Important Priorities for the following week.

- Try a communication exercise. Choose one of your direct reports. Hold a conversation in which you draw out their values and objectives and discuss how they connect to the values and objectives of your company, department or team.

- Make some notes and commitments to yourself on any of your personal issues that block effective time management. Consider these:

  —Disconnected Wildly Important Priorities (WIPs)

  —Perfectionism

  —A disorganized work area

  —Allowing excessive interruptions

  —Ineffective meetings

- Make three lists:

  1. What I do to manage my stress level

  2. What I could do that would be more helpful

  3. What I will do and when I will start

- Find someone who has been in management longer than you and discuss what you have learned here about the core beliefs that can dilute the effectiveness of even good managers—plus any others you may identify.

- Talk with the person you trust most about your style and motivations as a manager. Ask for their thoughts about how what they see confirms, and doesn't confirm, your self-knowledge.

- Tell your boss that you have read this book and are making a focused effort to learn and develop your management skills. Ask him or her to make two or three key suggestions and to recommend training.

The **3rd** Lever: Leadership

"The leader begins, then, by backing himself, inspiring himself, trusting himself, and ultimately inspires others by being trustworthy."

—Warren Bennis

Leadership is influence for change. Leaders open new paths and influence others to follow. Formal authority is a very limited source of influence. Wherever a person is on the organization chart, when he or she influences others for good, for productivity, for personal and career growth, for quality, for attitudes that contribute to a motivating environment that person has exercised leadership. Leadership is not a job. It is a function. Formal authority does not grant the ability to lead effectively. That ability is developed by managers reaching for greatness.

The authority of a manager to hire and fire does influence the performance of subordinates, but to a limited extent. It will get compliance. It will cause people to deliver the effort required to avoid termination. They will meet the minimum requirements of their job description. But this authority that is vested in managers will not guarantee the results that an organization needs. For that, you need a lever. Leadership is that potent lever.

Managers who use the lever of leadership are always calling upon others to stretch beyond "business as usual." They are not satisfied with implementing the plan that was written last year. Even a good plan can become a limiting container rather than an empowering facilitator of business success. Then-General Eisenhower knew a bit about planning. He planned the D-Day Invasion of Europe during the Second World War and was subsequently elected President of the United States. He said, "Plans are useless, but planning is indispensable." That's the voice of leadership.

Leadership is opportunity focused. It seeks robust adaptation rather than rigid conformance to a plan document. Information and adaptation are the real strategic advantages.

Great managers are not defenders of the way things are and have been. They always lead an organization to change for the better. The voice of leadership asks:

- What is a better way to move ahead?

- What should we do to cut costs, raise revenue and improve quality?

- Why does this same problem that we're facing today keep coming up in different dress month after month?

- How can I improve our relationships with our suppliers? And get a better price?

- Customer Y isn't calling on us as often. What's going on?

What distinguishes each of these, and a hundred more, from caretaker (business as usual) management is that each involves assessing the system and leading change. As has often been stated: Management is doing things right; leadership is doing the right things. Leadership uses a more wide-angle lens to understand the workings of a unit and applies energy to leverage change.

A job description describes what has been done in the past. It codifies for purposes of recruiting, hiring, orienting and guiding an employee. But the past is never good enough to enable a company to survive, thrive and grow into its preferred future. Competition changes. What customers want and expect changes. The economy changes. The regulatory environment changes.

Employees and managers who are limited to functioning within unchanging job descriptions and whose relationship is circumscribed by formal authority can never ensure the survival of the organization—let alone excellence.

Formal authority, job descriptions, your basket of management skills—these things will enable you to maintain the status quo, to keep the machinery oiled, and to oversee a static organization. But in the modern environment of a prosperous nation, the static organization is doomed. Effective managers need a lever for change.

Leadership is that lever.

So how do the skills of leadership and management relate? Who is a leader? Who grants the authority to lead? Does leadership have practices that can be described and learned?

LEADERSHIP AND MANAGEMENT

For a couple of decades, trainers and speakers seemed to be saying that management was a negative and leadership a positive. The implication was that people who aspire to be an authority for others should lead rather than manage. The truth is that management and leadership are practices that a great manager integrates. You can hear it in her voice. The voice of leadership affirms rather than defends. Great managers aspire to lead. Full integration of the practices of leadership and management is called for.

The voice of management says:

- Here is the budget we operate within

- This is the plan for how we will operate. I will expect you to follow it.

- These are the kinds of people we want to hire. Let's focus our search.

- Are you executing according to plan? What have been the results?

- What is compromising our ability to achieve our objectives, and how can I solve the problem?

- Are my direct reports working together constructively? If not, how can I intervene?

- Do our structures integrate well? If not, what is needed?

- What fires do I need to put out today?

The voice of leadership says:

- How is the cultural environment for our goods or services changing, and what changes does our organization need to make in order to move into our preferred future?

- Let's talk about our vision of our preferred and possible future

- That future is possible for us. It is worthy of your energy and passion. Let's go!

- Yes, there are obstacles, but you are the "A team." It's going to be all right.

Management is grounded in skills and practices. Its ultimate value is competence. Leadership is grounded in character and credibility. Its ultimate value is influence. Great managers lead the way to new places. They take their units to new levels of performance, to exceptional results. Their leadership makes that possible. Great managers wed competence and influence.

WHO GRANTS THE AUTHORITY TO LEAD?

"Change from the top down happens at the will and whim of those below," says Peter Block in *The Empowered Manager*. People will grant you the opportunity to lead when they have experienced that you are competent and trustworthy.

Enough said! Remember it.

THE PRACTICES OF LEADERSHIP

Being the change

Mahatma Gandhi, who knew a lot about leadership, said, "Be the change you want to see in the world." People don't follow your words, your techniques or even your skills. They follow you.

Probably you have noticed that in the first few minutes with a new acquaintance you form an impression of who they are, not just what they say. Perhaps there are occasions when this is unfair or you discover later that you were mistaken. But most of the time, it's a shortcut that saves the effort of weeks of observing and drawing conclusions. We even see this in early campaigning for elected officials. Without really knowing much at all about a candidate, we form an impression that seldom changes. "Yes, he could do the job." "He looks official." "I believe she has the right stuff."

There is mystery here. We don't have a word for what we are seeing that fully explains its power. We have many words. We say that he or she has presence, gravitas, style, looks the part or is genuine. We say that we have "a certain feeling" or a "hunch" about him or her.

What we are sensing in the other can best be called authenticity. We experience leaders as authentic when their thinking, their feeling and their behavior all pretty much go in the same direction. At least most of the time.

Some examples may serve to clarify:

- "He says he wants to hear from us, but what we say never really makes any difference. It's like he read somewhere that he should let people have their say."

- "She says she's all right with it … but you can tell she's mad as the devil."

- "Yeah, he dropped the bad news on us, but it was obvious that he took no pleasure in it."

- "She really meant it when she said she was going to be transparent. I'm surprised she shared that with us."

- "Yeah, he demands a lot, but he demands a lot of himself too. You can't help but respect him."

People will follow an authentic leader because they want more authenticity themselves. They will follow congruence because they long for more of it in their own lives. This is a potent factor in your use of the leadership lever. When you understand this, you can model the characteristics, the attitudes, the energy, the commitment and the styles of engaging people that you want to see people use on the job. People will do as you do, not as you say.

It's an old question—are leaders born, or can leadership be learned? Some people seem to have been born being comfortable in their own skin. From the time they are adolescents, groups look to them to lead. Others find that it takes some adult experience to discover their capacities and confidence. They come late to leadership. Probably for most, the full flowering of leadership springs from both: inborn leanings (though sometimes recognized late) and learning about human relations and the practices of leadership.

Since you have read this far, and have gotten yourself in a management position, it is a fair assumption that something about leadership appeals to you. You have some sense that this role is a natural fit. Explore that. Act on it. Observe how people respond. Ask for their feedback on what you do that helps and what they need. Listen. Learn to lead.

Building trusting relationships

Trust is like air. If you don't have it, you can't think of anything else. A leader who is not trusted is an oxymoron, like "large shrimp" and "civil war." You lose trust, you lose leadership.

> Trusting people has a powerful effect on them. Great managers have the attitude that the people they lead don't have to earn trust, they start with it. Giving trust positions you as a leader.

Leaders get trust by giving trust. How did you learn to be trustworthy? Someone trusted you, and they acknowledged it when you respected it and handled their trust well. That built a valued connection of mutual trust between you. You valued the connection so much that you became trustworthy in order to preserve it.

Leaders get trust by being trustworthy. Very soon, your subordinates will know whether you say what you mean, mean what you say and do what you say you will do.

Trust rests on candor and transparency:

- **Candor**—tell it as it is with a minimum of politically correct fluff

- **Transparency**—few secrets. Tell them what you are up to, what you value, what you expect, how you expect accountability, what is going well and what is not. Admit mistakes and shortfalls.

Building a common vision that inspires and calls out people's best contribution

A vision is not an idea. It's not even a good idea. It's a compelling image of a preferred and possible future.

In the play *Dancing at Lughnasa*, Michael is a seven-year-old boy who is being raised by his mother and her four sisters in a small village in Ireland. His unreliable father has left Michael and his mother to fend for themselves. Gerry, the father, comes back for a visit.

There is a moving scene where the father is trying to give his son an understanding of the wider world, its excitement and possibilities. He pretends that he has a bird in his hand, tells Michael how wonderful the bird and its flight are, opens his hands, looks up in amazement and asks Michael if he saw it.

People who can cast a vision help us see beyond concrete reality and feel the possibilities in imagination, life and work. They show what is not yet real and inspire us to see it with them. We follow those people.

You probably have such a vision. You can look down the road of your organization and your unit in it and imagine what the future could hold. The people who report to you already have a vision. If you asked them, "When you look down the road a year or two, what do you think our unit will be like?" they probably would have an answer.

Your task as leader is clear and sequential. You can't afford to neglect any step in the sequence:

1. Draw out their vision; get them talking about it

2. Lay your vision alongside theirs. Describe it in ways that show that you really, really care about it.

3. Keep talking until you create a shared vision together

4. Use your influence to infuse it with realistic hope

5. Create a clear line of sight between the vision and the tasks today, this month, this year

A leader is someone people are willing to follow. If you think you are leading and look around to find that no one is following, you're not leading, you are just strolling around. Managers who can cast a vision that holds value, meaning and a connection to the wish that people have to make a significant contribution will find followers.

What is your vision of the preferred and possible future of your organization and the unit you lead? Can you describe it to others in ways that magnetize attention and passion?

Many organizations write a vision statement, post it on the wall, laminate it on a card and forget it. Make your vision a living thing that helps you manage. Here are some things you can do that that will make that possible:

1. Spend some quiet time in reflection and complete the following sentences in writing:

   - We're going to be an organization that …
   - We're going to be the kind of place to work where people …
   - We're going to have …
   - We're going to provide …

2. Practice communicating these ideas. Find someone outside your workplace whom you can practice with. Look them in the eye and in thirty seconds tell them your vision for your unit.

3. Once you have a shared vision with your team, talk about it all the time with the people you lead. Sending out a memo, writing it in the policy manual, putting it on a poster in the break room or mentioning it in a couple of meetings will not get the job done. You want to talk about it every day until you are afraid that they will run you out of town if you say it again.

4. So that you don't have to leave town, develop a hundred different ways to talk about it. Tell the vision. It's great! It's beautiful! And it's possible!

5. Make sure that your vision is reflected in your performance expectations and your rewards.

Building a powerful motivating environment

There is much talk, often by frustrated managers, about how to motivate and empower people. Some managers unintentionally create an environment that jerks the rug out from under motivation and empowerment. You can disempower people by not listening to them, discounting their efforts, taking personal credit for their accomplishments, using a command and control style, and failing to acknowledge outstanding contributions. But there are things you can't do.

> You can't motivate people. You can't empower them. Leaders *can* build a motivational environment in which people can motivate and empower themselves. Treat everyone as a source of creative input.

Empowerment is about having voice and choice. Managers look for ways to call out the voice of those doing the core work of an organization. Managers look for ways to invite them to make choices. Having voice and choice, most people will empower themselves to use them.

In every training workshop I have ever conducted for managers, when we discuss empowerment, someone asks, "Yeah, but what if your people won't … " Yes, there are people who will not, or cannot, respond to even the best attempts of a leader to build a motivating environment. If the motivating environment is present and people cannot or will not motivate themselves, don't frustrate yourself or waste your time. Decide whether their contribution is at least adequate. If not, there is a conversation that you must have. You can't control anyone's internal reality. And it's not the job of management to reconstruct a resistant or toxic employee's personality.

Leading by building a motivating environment, you will:

- Ask what your direct reports think. Listen and value their insights.

- Praise people and avoid direct personal criticism where others can hear

- Reward accomplishments

- Voice the opportunities and solutions while acknowledging the problems

- Feed the strengths and starve the weaknesses

One of the global leaders in the office furniture industry seeks and uses the input of machine operators when a new machine must be designed. They will not start production of the new piece of equipment until the person who will operate it has reviewed the design, suggested modifications and finally approved the machine. Then, when the new equipment is delivered, there is a brass plate engraved with the name of the operator.

The company does not go to this trouble because they are nice people, though perhaps they are. They know the benefit, to company and individuals, of building a positive motivational environment.

Challenging the way things are done

There is a popular saying, "If it ain't broke, don't fix it." Managers using the leadership lever have another saying, "If it ain't broke, fix it anyway."

Leaders don't wait until the operating system is broken, or until its inadequacy is obvious to everyone, to fix or improve it. Leaders have a prevailing curiosity that is always asking, "I wonder if there is a better way to do this?" They ask the people nearest to the job the same question because they understand that the person nearest the work is the one best prepared to understand and improve it. They actively challenge the notion that "Good enough is good enough."

In his book, *Winning*, Jack Welch, retired CEO of General Electric, tells of a procedure he developed called a "Work-Out Process" which led to an explosion in their productivity and brought every brain into the game. As a routine way of solving problems, groups were brought together to talk, confidentially and without their managers present, about better ways to do things and how to break through roadblocks that were hindering them. Toward the end of the meetings, the managers would return and follow through on the promise to give an immediate yes or no answer to seventy-five percent of the recommendations. Then, over the next thirty days, the managers would resolve the other twenty-five percent.

Leaders think like that.

Building confidence

This may be job one for managers using the leadership lever. The bedrock of most people's self-confidence is their ability to solve problems on their own. Leaders take every opportunity to acknowledge (mention it where others can hear) that a person has done this.

- Express your appreciation for a job well done

- Spread an infectious attitude that says, "We can do this. And you can make a great contribution!"

- Create opportunities to celebrate even small achievements along the way without waiting for ultimate victory. Use your sense of humor.

In the 90's, I was managing a unit that badly needed to increase its customer base. At a meeting one Friday, I announced with mock seriousness, "We're instituting a new incentive program today. Anyone lands a contract with a new company—the rest of us are going to wax their car and baby sit their children for a week."

The marketing manager, who really didn't like children at all, raised his hand and volunteered, "I'll wax the cars!"

When the laughter died down, we established a ritual of the "Car Wax Award." Anytime someone landed a new contract, we called everyone together and with great fanfare presented them a can of car wax. Everyone had fun with it.

Managers who aspire to lead understand that enormous doors swing on such small hinges.

Action Steps You Can Take

Leadership is not a quality that you either have or you don't. It's not a skill established once and for all like riding a bicycle. It is a lever, a practice that you will want to nurture and cultivate across your entire career in management.

Good to Great author Jim Collins and his team analyzed 28 companies that made and sustained a leap from good to great for at least fifteen years. Their finding that leadership had a lot to do with the abiding success of these companies is not surprising. However, they were surprised to discover the type of leadership required. Collins calls it "Level Five Leadership," and sees it as the culmination of a process that takes a maturing manager/leader through four previous levels:

- Highly capable individual
- Contributing team member
- Competent manager
- Effective leader

A Level Five leader is described as "an individual who blends extreme personal humility with intense professional will."

What is meant by "professional will" here is a driving ambition for success and exceptional performance by the organization. The attribution of humility may conflict with the popular image of a leader. But Collins' research is very compelling.

Intense will is not often coupled with extreme personal humility. Perhaps that is why the leadership that builds and sustains greatness in a company for at least fifteen years is as rare as it is.

If you aspire to exceptional leadership, here are some things you could do:

- Since true humility is an often-neglected quality in our culture, take the measure of your humility. Are you more interested in leading a great unit or looking good? Do you credit others for your success and take personal responsibility for your failures, or is it the other way around? Is it harder for you to cultivate your humility or your will?

- Identify a leader you know who has the qualities of a Level Five leader. How did they become level five? Talk with them. See what you can learn from them.

- If you are early in your management career, look for the opportunity to work with someone who has the reputation of being a great leader. Seeing it is more helpful than hearing about it.

- Read the best books you can find on leadership. Attend training and be an active participant. Be deliberate about cultivating your gift of leadership. Don't leave it to chance, believing that time and experience will take care of it. You will need to take care of it.

The 4th Lever: Facilitating the Life Cycle of Employees

A futurist, attempting humor, once said that as technology and automation progress the factory of the future will only have a machine, one manager and a dog. The manager's job would be to monitor the dials on the machine. The dog's job would be to keep the manager from touching the machine. Fortunately, technology has not yet been able to remove the human element in work.

You do not manage a thing, a machine. You manage a living, organic creation, an organization that moves forward on the energy and commitment of people. The results of the organization are in the hands of individuals who have drives, ups and downs, aspirations, and who get irritated from time to time. A new manager who was beginning to feel this reality joked with his manager, "You told me I would have human resources, but what I got was people! And they each have one of those little things called a personality!"

Great managers keep learning to develop and integrate their business skills and their people skills. If you cannot keep one eye on the bottom line and the other on the needs of people, you might want to consider working in bookkeeping or counseling rather than in management.

Employees have a life cycle in an organization. They enter, they get connected to the corporate culture, they exercise their gifts, they develop maturing competence (or not), and they leave—by their own initiative or that of a manager. Managers are privileged to facilitate employees' transitions through this life cycle.

The journey is personal, and a facilitative manager is needed. The depth and complexity of the process can be appreciated by looking at the parallels with the human life cycle generally:

- Entering (by hiring)—Birth
- Getting connected to the culture—Childhood
- Exercising their talents—Early adulthood
- Developing maturing competence—Later adulthood
- Separating—Death

If the word death seems too harsh a metaphor for leaving employment, remember that when employees leave these are often occasions involving a range of similar emotions: shock, grief, anger, anxiety and relief.

Great managers understand that working in the employment life cycle involves a skill much more sophisticated and human than just filling out the proper forms that expedite the transitions. They use a lever called facilitation.

Facilitation involves making a process easier, or at least less difficult. A second common meaning relates to assisting the progress of a person. Managers work to facilitate the transitions in this life cycle—to make them easier for the employee, the organization and themselves.

The typical life cycle of an employee has changed over the years. The average employment life cycle today is quite different than your grandfather's. The age is gone when loyalty between organization and employee was strong, when moves across a continent were less frequent, when defined-benefit retirement plans were enriched by longevity, when families were more stable, when job security meant more than upward mobility in the job market and when employees were less likely to sue. That age is gone, or is going.

The employment life cycle has shortened, become more complex and more demanding of the time and skill of managers. Great managers work to find, hire and retain people who will stay longer, develop capacity over a period of years and make a more valuable contribution than in the early years. It is a large order.

Fortunately, you have an ally in your organization's Human Resources Department. Cultivate that relationship. Some managers resist this invitation. They have a wide streak of independence and an attitude that says, "Just let me manage my unit. I can handle it thank you very much." While this attitude may be understandable from the perspective of personality, it is short sighted and risky from a business perspective. The HR Department can make your working life easier and cover your assets, defending them against great loss.

Jack Welch writes in his chapter on people management, "Elevate HR to a position of power and primacy in the organization, and make sure HR people have the special qualities to help managers build leaders and careers. In fact, the best HR types are pastors and parents in the same package."

THE COVENANT BETWEEN EMPLOYER AND EMPLOYEE

Formal contracts are put in writing and are legally enforceable. The older words (covenant, concord and compact) better describe the relationship managers have with employees. Expectations and mutual conditional promises are exchanged, usually orally, and are renegotiated over time.

The older covenant was expressed in the phrase "an honest day's work for an honest day's pay." While that is still a legitimate expectation, both employers and employees now expect more. In the highly competitive, rapidly changing, knowledge-based work culture, the mantra is "More. More. More."

Employers look for people who will aspire to more than the minimum requirements for continued employment. They want people who are looking for a career, not just a job. They want people who will make themselves more valuable to the organization next year than this year. They want performance and ethical behavior.

Employees are looking for contributions to their life and career as well as to their checkbook. They want to learn something while working with you that will make them more valuable in the workplace. They want a positive work environment with colleagues that are constructive. They want a manager who will be more of a coach than a referee.

The manager's job is to find as much of what is wanted as possible and to offer as much as is reasonable without setting the new employee up for disappointment and disillusionment if the organization cannot deliver on the offer.

Both employer and employee are best served by candor and transparency about the likely experience they will have together. A good deal that is not a good deal for everybody will fall apart. If someone you have decided to offer a job would be joining a unit that faces steep challenges, requires rigorous effort and has some inexperienced employees—tell them so. If it scares them off, maybe that is for the best. Maybe it's better and less expensive to lose them now than it would be a few months down the road. You are looking for someone who will rise to this challenge.

ENTERING THE ORGANIZATION

Recruiting

As culture and the culture of work evolve and become more complex and demanding, managers are aware that the available talent pool is not as rich as they might like. There is not an army of star performers waiting to apply at most organizations.

Your recruitment efforts do not begin by posting the availability of a job in your organization's communication network or the public media. Long before a specific opening becomes available, you have a reputation in the community that shapes your stream of likely applicants. Some of that reputation has been shaped by the people who have left you in the past. Build an architecture for work and a motivational environment where people work hard because they want to, and word gets around. They say things to their neighbors, their family and their communities:

> "Yes, that's a great place to work. They treat you fairly. I learned a lot while I was with them."

> Or,

> "Well, you might want to think long and hard before you apply there."

As you prepare to recruit for a new employee, you can prepare for a more successful search by listing three things:

1. **Characteristics of the star performers in your unit.** Every unit in an organization has its own cultural identity, spirit and way that individuals work together. Over time this influences and defines the characteristics of the people who are most positive and productive there. Considering their qualities will make it more likely that you will hire people who will be compatible with your workforce and become star performers themselves.

2. **Core competencies.** What are the essential competencies required for adequate performance in the position? Must the applicant be able to design computer programs, negotiate contracts, sell goods or services, write reports summarizing business efforts and results, facilitate telephone communications, receive visitors well or something else?

As you make your list, don't rely on a job description that was written four years ago. This may be the time to update the description. Jobs evolve, and competencies increase or decrease in importance.

3. **Personal qualities** (ethics, energy, intelligence, people and communication skills). Regardless of how proficient an individual is in the core competencies, the lack of these personal qualities will severely compromise their value to an organization.

Managers decide how much weight to give to core competencies and how much to give to personal qualities. Some managers have said that it is wise to hire for character and train for skills. This is probably good advice when the required skills are not at a high level of technical or professional functioning (such as networking computers within a large organization or performing surgery, for example).

Interviewing

First, seek the guidance of your Human Resources department. Follow the procedures laid down by the policy of your organization. General guidelines that are included in the policies of most organizations include:

- Follow the same procedure and use the same documented questions with each applicant

- Use a small group rather than an individual interviewer. Have each record their evaluation of an applicant's response to each question and average their responses for a final score.

- Show each applicant a copy of the job description for the position and ask if they have questions or concerns

- Do not ask questions that are unlawful. Seek the guidance of your Human Resources Department.

- Never allow unlawful discrimination to become a part of your evaluation of applicants

    Most managers will admit to having biases. A bias is just a preference. A manager said, "Other things being equal, I would rather hire somebody forty-five than hire somebody twenty-five." The fact that this manager is conscious of her bias enables her to guard against letting it become a prejudice that leads to unlawful discrimination. Pre-judging based on a personal bias is the risk.

- After you have made a selection, inform each applicant in writing. If someone was not selected, do not say why they were not. Simply thank them for their application and state that the position has been offered to another applicant.

The best predictor of future success is past success. There are interview questions that will let you reap the benefit of this insight:

- Tell us about some of your proudest accomplishments in previous jobs

- Tell us about a time when you had a strong disagreement with your manager. How did you handle it and how did it come out?

- Tell us about a time when you were burdened by multiple projects and responsibilities. How did you handle it and how did it end up?

- Why did you leave your last job? Or why are you considering leaving?

- What kind of manager do you need?

I particularly like the questions that ask applicants to tell about their experiences that were challenging rather than asking them what they think about how challenging experiences should be handled. Most applicants have read a book or article on how to interview and anticipate how they will answer some questions. Talking about specific experiences may give you a passport to reality.

Go into the interview process with the attitude that you are trying to facilitate the entry of the right person into your organization, not trying to screen out the wrong people. This will allow you to provide an atmosphere in which applicants can demonstrate their strengths rather than attempt to conceal their weaknesses. People do not excel in the workplace because they overcome their weaknesses. They excel because they use their strengths in a unit where those strengths are the ones most needed. Look for their strengths. What could they do?

GETTING CONNECTED TO THE CULTURE

The first few days and early months of a new employee's tenure have parallels with childhood. Perhaps you can remember when you were a child and moved into a new neighborhood or started at a new school. It was a time surrounded with some anxiety. It presented an opportunity to form new relationships that had the potential (but not the guarantee) to become important and supportive. It carried an opportunity to show who you were, what you liked and what you could do.

Parents and teachers facilitate the resolution of the anxiety into prudent risk-taking and self-revealing. In the workplace, managers do the same thing. Here are some things to consider doing:

Introductions

Introduce the new employee to everyone they will work with on a regular basis. Provide an interesting hook that the established employee can relate to, not just the name of the new employee. Briefly describe what the new employee will be dong that will be valuable.

New employee orientation programs

If your organization has a formally conducted orientation program, you will want to participate. If not, you will need to structure one yourself. You begin by asking yourself some questions:

- What are our mission, vision, values and ethical bedrock? What is our product, service and brand, and what is its value to the culture?

- What are our Wildly Important Priorities, and how do they connect to the large goals of the organization?

- What are the core skills we use, and what resources are available to develop proficiency?

- What are the obligations and opportunities of teamwork? How does one unit relate to and support the work of others?

- What are the structures for accountability for results?

- Other questions that are particular to your organization

Whether you cover these foundations in a formally designed program for everyone or discuss them at length with new people individually, it is time well spent. Avoid any rush you may feel to get a warm body on the front line and functioning. Pay the price for better performance down the road.

Facilitate a quick success

Assign the new employee to a task where quick, and visible, success is likely. When the success comes, mention it where others can hear. Groups of employees will value what you value, and first impressions tend to last.

Assign a peer guide

Introduce this person to the new employee as someone who "for the first month will help you get a feel for how we do things here." When you select this person, you want someone who knows the ropes and will convey a positive attitude.

Stay close

Without hovering, be more available early on than you usually are. Signal that you want the employee to feel free to look you up with any questions or concerns. Ask how things are going.

EXERCISING THEIR TALENTS

Great managers match what needs to be done with employees' skills and interests. After an employee has been with you for a few months, or after you have been managing a new group for that long, you have a fairly clear idea of an individual's talents that will contribute the most to your organization. You have the opportunity—through job assignments, delegation of tasks or projects and forming teams—to position people where they will enjoy what they are doing and the organization will get the best bang for the buck.

Match the job's characteristics and the individual's skills and interests. The door that opens to this practice is the conversation with the employee in which you ask them to tell you the kinds of work they love and the kinds they are good at. What they like and what they are good at are not necessarily the same things. Very talented people can be good at a great variety of tasks that they do not necessarily enjoy. Be sure that you know your people well enough to make the best use of their gifts. Good wages and job security will do little to overcome the negative effects of individuals feeling that their abilities are not understood and are being underutilized.

Much management research has shown that the most powerful contributor to the retention of good employees is the nature of the job itself, not the office with a window, perks or even salary.

Since productivity that goes beyond the minimum comes down to attitude, have people work at things they feel draw on their gifts and are worthy of their best effort. People are more likely to deliver peak performance if they love what they are doing. They stay in jobs, thereby reducing turnover costs, because they become involved in work that is consistent with their long-held, deeply embedded interests. Match the tasks you need to have done with the people who will do them best.

No manager has the luxury of putting everybody to work, all the time, on things they love to do. There are things that must be done whether anybody loves them or not. You can't keep everybody happy by having them do only the work they love. But when they know you are respectful of their individuality, you gain respect as a leader.

These interventions are called job redesign and job matching, and the results are impressive. Using these interventions, for example, the U.S. Social Security Administration increased productivity 23.5% among a group of fifty employees. General Electric realized a 50% increase in product quality in one unit, and the absenteeism rate among data-processing operators at Travelers Insurance decreased by 24%.

DEVELOPING MATURING COMPETENCE

You want people in your unit who will take responsibility for developing their capacities and become stronger contributors next year than this. You screen for this in your selection and hiring process, and you get a fuller appraisal of it in their early months of employment. "John, what do you aspire to? What do you want out of your career? Out of your life? What do you want to learn while you're working here?"

Great managers usually enjoy this aspect of managing—bringing others along to advanced levels of competence and self-fulfillment. It is a great legacy to leave. But always be clear, with yourself and with them, that the prime responsibility for development is theirs, not yours.

Remember the old saying "When the student is ready the teacher appears." You cannot develop someone who is not ready or willing.

Reading Stephen R. Covey's *The 7 Habits of Highly Effective People* enabled me to take a large step forward. But not before I was ready. The year it was published, I was in a bookstore, saw this title and realized that some of my friends had been talking about it. I bought it and read the first two chapters during the flight. I really wondered what all the buzz was about. This was nothing new—just the common wisdom of mankind with some applications to the world of work.

Upon arriving home, I realized that I had left the book in a phone booth. I wasn't ready. Sigmund Freud said that events like this are not accidents, but are the work of the unconscious.

A couple of years later, a university intern student was packing up at the end of the internship and said to me, "I found two copies of this book on my shelf so you can have one of them." He handed me *The 7 Habits of Highly Effective People*. I took it home that night and again read the first two chapters. This time, it blew me out of the water. It tore me out of my frame of reference about my life and work. I was ready.

Great managers make it their business to challenge and develop people, enabling them to build capacity, learn new skills and become more confident. Managers have at their disposal an array of practices that contribute to the development of the people they lead.

Training

Training is not a development program. Don't let yourself think that just because you have sent someone to a training program you have satisfied their development initiative for that year. Training can provide a strong contribution to a person's development program, but it is not the whole thing. Think of it as valuable and necessary, but not all-inclusive.

There are two ways you can ensure that you reap the benefits of training:

1. Prepare an employee before he attends a training event and follow up afterward.

2. Use your organization's training service to help your unit respond to operational challenges.

Most organizations do not do these things. As a result, training is regarded as an expense, not a service that adds value to the enterprise. Training becomes a social occasion, a break from and reward for hard work, rather than a strong contributor to business results. Often operating managers have seen the training function in their organization as taking employees away from productive time or meddling in the operating manager's domain.

You can change this perception and by that action increase your value to your organization.

When you are ready to send a direct report to an external training event, first have a conversation that runs something like this:

> Beth, I want you to attend this training next month. I believe it will help you with some of the things you and I have been discussing. What I want you to learn is_____. And when you come back, I'd like you to prepare a 30-minute presentation for the rest of our group summarizing for them what you learned. And then you and I will coach some of them for a few weeks. Then we will evaluate together how things are going and whether we're improving. OK?

An intervention something like this turns a corner into a new reality. Training begins to produce operational results. Expectations are raised. Outcomes improve.

Many organizations are giving their old-fashioned Training Department a new name— Performance Improvement Department. Changing the name does not accomplish the desired change, but it is a symbolic act that announces an intention and can therefore enlist targeted action.

When you experience an operational challenge that is not responding to your usual coaching, talk with the person responsible for training/performance improvement.

Ask them to help you think about the kind of intervention that can yield operational results. Explore together your desired results, the actual results you are getting, what may be in the performance gap and what could be done. Skilled professionals in training/performance improvement are prepared to help you consider a variety of possible interventions:

- Job analysis and possible restructuring

- Work-flow between individuals or units and how it could be improved

- A training seminar. If this is the intervention of choice, participate with the designer of the training to define objectives, design training that will best meet them and plan for post-training coaching back on the job. When designing in-house training involves the manager who is responsible for results, and the training is followed up with supervision, mentoring and coaching that support the evolution of skill, the money for training is well invested. Without post-training coaching, nothing much will have changed six weeks later.

You will make a stronger contribution to these objectives if you attend the training with the people who work with you.

Use your director of training and performance improvement as an internal consultant.

Delegating tasks that will stretch people

There is no better way to develop people than to give them tasks, projects or short-term team assignments that call for them to develop new skills or improve existing ones. Experience, and reflection on it, is a powerful developer of capacity.

From time to time there will be people in your unit who have the potential to develop and move into management responsibility. You can move these people around, perhaps even to a short-term assignment in another unit, as a way of continuing to evaluate their management potential and expose them to the broad view of the entire organization.

Mentoring assignments

When you want to assist a person to develop competence in a particular function, you can assign them to a mentoring relationship with someone who has developed advanced competence. You will find that this develops both the mentor and the person being mentored.

Mentors introduce a person to new domains of relationship and competence. They have "been there and done that." They are prepared to show the way to someone who is relatively inexperienced by comparison. In assigning a mentor, you are looking for someone who enjoys a teaching relationship that is somewhat like parenting, but don't stretch that comparison too far.

Recommended reading

I know a man who is regarded internationally as an authority on the application of a technology to his industry that he had borrowed from another. I once asked him how he discovered and developed that possibility. He said, "I read." For your self-development, and that of the people who work with you, read and recommend it.

Building confidence

You have the opportunity to recognize important skills and achievements and comment on them. This is a powerful confidence builder. People are not always aware of their gifts. I had a manager once who became my mentor, then my friend. He said one day, "Did you know that you are good at taking things that come up in your individual coaching sessions with people and continuing to help with the same issue in group meetings in ways that don't leave them feeling that you have betrayed a confidence?"

No, I didn't know that at the time. But his noticing and naming it has helped me practice it more deliberately and more adequately ever since.

Writing

Ask an employee who has some good ideas to put them in writing for you and to include suggestions about how the ideas could be implemented. Again, this is a confidence builder, but it also can develop their skill of written communication.

The goal of all of these development initiatives is to discover what a person does well, what they could do well and weaknesses that block the full use of those strengths. Managers want to make the strengths of the people who work with them effective and construct an architecture for work where the weaknesses don't matter. Feed the strengths. Starve the weaknesses.

SEPARATING

Turnover is generally regarded as a problem by managers. It produces work. New applicants for a vacancy must be found. Interviews held. Decisions made. It costs time and money.

But some turnover is a good thing. New blood helps renew an organization. New people bring a vitality that sometimes calls established people forward. New ideas are put into the mix.

People who have grown with you and moved on to another organization when you do not have room to promote them will carry the message of the good experience they had with you. Their ability to speak well of your experience together is worth something to your organization. When someone comes to see you to announce that they are leaving, you want to:

- Congratulate them on having a new opportunity

- Wish them well

- Conduct a termination interview

- Indicate, if you mean it, that the door is open for them to come back and talk with you about reemployment if the new opportunity does not work out

When you conduct a good termination interview, you will learn a lot that will help you going forward. People often are able to say things when leaving that they have not been able to say before. You can focus your termination interview in a series of questions:

- What are you glad for in your experience working with us?

- What do you wish could have been different?

- What suggestions do you have for our improvement?

- What are you hoping for in your next job?

As they express the positives, they lay claim to them more fully and become more likely to tell others outside your organization. As they express the negatives directly to you, they become less likely to have to tell others. Expression of negatives reduces, rather than magnifies, their power.

When you must separate someone

Most managers find separating people from employment the most distasteful task in managing. It is also one of the most risky. Wrongful termination exposes you and your organization to the possibility of adverse action in court. Therefore, the first principle of critical importance is for a manager to walk through this process step-by-step with the Human Resources Department. They are your in-house experts in employment law and your best support and protection.

One general management principle is observed in the policy of all organizations. Be sure that you have provided coaching, prior to the decision to terminate, that pointed out the precise areas of inadequate performance, indicated required improvement and made clear the possible costs (up to and including termination) of continued nonperformance. Be sure that you have documented those interviews.

Most organizations provide for a sequence of interventions, progressing in severity as the possibility of termination comes closer: supervisory conferences, a verbal warning, a written warning and a well-conducted termination interview. Most organizations also provide for more abrupt termination in the event of severe violation of policy or law.

One organization where I managed had a policy allowing a unique intervention that I have seen nowhere else. Managers who had tried everything else to save a resistant employee were allowed to tell them that they were to take two days off with pay and that when they returned the manager either wanted them to sign in and become a strong contributor or resign. I have seen this save a couple of good people.

There is a phrase that is worth a lot as you engage the progressive discipline process. When the time is right, you describe the person's nonperformance. Then you describe their assets: "Mike, you have a lot you could offer here. I don't want to lose you." This lets him know that it has crossed your mind that you might have to terminate his employment. It also attributes to him the power to avoid termination.

Most of the problems managers experience in terminating people lie in the manager's attitudes and emotions. Dread of conflict and anticipated guilt cause far too many managers to tolerate then terminate. Too much inadequate performance is tolerated for too long. Then one day the manager gets "up to here" and abruptly fires the employee, often without going through the proper procedures.

A manager's personal feelings and attitudes are particularly likely to get in the way when an employee may be involved in substance abuse or dependency. A manager's personal values in this area, not to mention feelings about his own pattern of use, can turn the manager aside from the task of management. When this happens, there is a risk that the manager will begin acting out of the role of a counselor or investigator.

Managers do not assess or diagnose substance-related problems. It is not a manager's responsibility to get the facts about an employee's pattern of use. It is the manager's responsibility to manage for performance. Harmful involvement in substances will negatively impact performance. The performance issue then becomes the proper focus of management's attention and response.

If a manager feels that the use of substances may be causing the performance problem, the proper intervention sounds something like this:

> "Grace, you know my concern about your performance recently. And I don't see it improving. Since you have the skills, and have in the past had the drive, I'm wondering if there is some personal concern that is harming your effectiveness. It's not my business to pry into your personal life, but if it's something personal, I hope you will do whatever it takes to address it. I don't want to lose you. You may want to see a counselor if you're under personal stress. But whether you do or not, I have no alternative but to hold you responsible for the quality of your work."

If at that point the employee acknowledges a problem with excessive substance use, don't be drawn into trying to diagnose it or prescribe things they could do about it. Avoid professional terms like "addicted" or "alcoholic." You might instead say, "Well, it sounds like this thing could be important. I hope you will see a professional who could help you with it." Some managers keep a list of two or three personal counselors or psychologists that they can share with employees who request a referral. When they are aware that the problem is substance related, they often refer to a credentialed substance-abuse professional.

You can help yourself with your personal discomfort over terminating employment by being clear with yourself about two things:

1. People fire themselves

2. You are paid to manage

When you follow good management practices and the policies of your organization, you have brought a nonperforming employee to clear awareness of the concerns, what they must do to address them and the potential consequences if they do not. If they then do not, it is clear evidence that they are either unable or unwilling to do so. In either case, they have brought themselves to a place where your organization no longer can afford to keep them—they have fired themselves. Good management practices ensure that people will not be surprised when they come to a termination interview.

Keep the termination interview brief and to the point. Do not allow it to degenerate into lengthy discussion or argument about the justification for your action. That discussion already has taken place. Inform the person of your decision, the effective date and time (the sooner the better) and the procedure regarding any accumulated benefits, and wish them well. You may choose to have a third party from Human Resources participate in the interview. This is particularly wise if you expect any anger that could escalate into aggressive behavior.

Yes, all of this is uncomfortable for you—especially when your organization is having to lay people off because of financial constraints. You may then have to terminate someone who is performing adequately. But you are paid to manage. Your prime responsibility is for the well-being of the organization. Fasten your sear belt. Support the employee through their transition and move on.

Your group will be impacted when anyone leaves them. Thoughts and feelings will be as diverse as the personalities involved. You will need to communicate something to them. Be brief with the facts. Take a little more time with the feelings. When someone has resigned, tell your group that they took the initiative in order to take another opportunity. When the organization is having to lay people off, tell your group so and resist any temptation to offer more reassurance about the future than you realistically can. When you have had to terminate someone, say so but do not discuss the reasons. They probably already know.

Allow your group to vent any feelings they have about the termination. It is an occasion of loss, even when some may be glad for the loss. Simply acknowledge the reality of the feelings, announce any plans to fill the vacant position and express your expectation that, though it is challenging, the group will continue their good work. Then, if you have the option, move to fill the vacancy with a strong applicant as soon as possible. This will reassure your group.

Facilitating the life-cycle of a group that works together is challenging, but very rewarding. Great managers empower themselves to ease the transitions in people's lives. They introduce them to new opportunities, show where their talents can best be put to use, help bring them to advanced competence and help them face uncomfortable truths.

Action Steps You Can Take

To empower yourself for using this lever, here are some things you can do:

- Which employee life cycle transition is most challenging for you to facilitate? Reflect on the issues and needs and make a commitment to yourself to learn and become more skilled in it over the next year.

- Finish this sentence and make some notes, "To develop my working relationship with our Human Resources department and become more skilled in those areas where we must work closely together, I probably need to … "

- Write out a two-minute description of your unit that you would want to share with someone you are recruiting. What satisfactions could they anticipate? What challenges? What kind of working relationship with you and with peers? After writing it, practice delivering it orally. Use it.

- Are there jobs under your management that need to be redesigned? If the last couple of people in a job have failed, this may strongly support a positive answer to that question. Or are there opportunities to construct a better match between some of the people in your unit and the tasks? Make some decisions.

- Decide what you will do to get a better return on the investment of your training dollars. Make some notes. Who do you need to talk with about this?

- Who in your unit could benefit from being a mentor or being mentored? Decide how you will initiate the process.

- Tell your manager that you are going to make a concentrated effort to improve your management skills over the next year and ask for some recommended readings

The 5th Lever: Accountability

Accountability is self-imposed in relationships of trust or it never becomes real.

Great managers let subordinates struggle with genuine responsibility for execution. Without this, you only have obedience, not accountability. And obedience must be re-imposed every time—it never gets internalized.

A fine manager I was coaching told me the story of his working relationship with his shift supervisor when he was working as a tower-based air traffic controller at a U.S. Air Force base. A fighter jet and a commercial passenger liner were both preparing to land. Their timing and paths would not guarantee Federal Aviation Administration (FAA) minimum separation requirements. If they pursued their direction and speed, they would probably collide.

The shift supervisor saw, and knew that the future manager I was coaching saw, the tragedy in the making. Only moments remained to avert disaster …

Air traffic controller: "What do you think?"

Shift supervisor: "I'm going to get some coffee. Let me know if they crash."

The controller handled it. They didn't crash. Two weeks later, when the shift supervisor left the position, he promoted the traffic controller to be shift supervisor.

In this watershed experience, the future manager learned the crucial lesson about establishing the ability of direct reports to hold themselves accountable. The willingness of his shift supervisor to not fix it for him, to permit him to struggle with decision and execution, to let him feel the full weight of responsibility provided a teachable moment that would resonate for a lifetime.

Accountability is the royal road to peak performance. It is the lever you use to help people take their performance from inadequate to good enough, then from good enough to exceptional and then to sustain the change over time.

Without the lever of accountability, all your good ideas about mission, vision, values, priorities and strategy are just that—good ideas. Managers put legs under good ideas. They send them out to change efforts and results. They understand that ideas are powerful, but only if they degenerate into work.

Among organizations that do not excel, the reason often comes down to lack of accountability. How is it possible to understand the glaring omission of so basic a requirement for execution? The roots of the omission reach down into two things.

1. **Unstructured permissiveness based in the manager's personal struggle with being an authority.**

   Strange as it may seem, some managers have difficulty holding people accountable for commitments. A manager said, "What troubles me is not our turnover rate. Actually, it is pretty good. What troubles me is the people we've lost who are still with us—people who have retired on the job."

   Some anticipate resentment from employees. Some fear setting team members in competition with one another or demoralizing them. Some fear that they will not be supported by more senior managers. The personal reasons are as diverse as the managers caught in this trap. If you identify any of this issue in your own career, you may want to go back and re-read the section on authority over, authority with and authority for in Lever One.

2. **Misunderstanding of what accountability is.**

   Accountability is not a principle managers use to control people. Short of prison, no one can successfully control another for very long. Control destroys a relationship.

   Great managers seek to influence people who can then manage themselves for self-actualization and contribution to shared objectives.

   Accountability is a dynamic in a relationship that facilitates personal growth and accomplishment. Think about your own achievements. Did you achieve them in isolation or in relationships with others who expected you to achieve, contributed something to your efforts and celebrated the achievements with you? Some things can be accomplished alone. But these are not usually the great things.

I have a very bright friend who has a Ph.D. in psychology and for a while worked as a consultant. He confessed to me one day that he is not very self-directing, self-motivating. I asked him how it was possible that he got his doctorate. My impression was that getting an advanced degree requires sustained self-direction over a significant period of time. My friend explained that in a doctoral program there are milestones along the way for which you are held accountable.

My friend was not describing a character flaw so much as a fundamental reality. People discover their full potential and bring it from bud to flower. They accomplish more, they enjoy the journey more in relationships of accountability.

I have another very able friend who spent his very satisfying career not in management but in low-level assignments, making adequate but undistinguished contributions. He said, "I have studiously clawed and scratched my way to the bottom." It satisfied him. He was happy. But more is required of managers. Organizations need managers who will keep their hand on the plow and their eyes ever toward the horizon.

Managers structure relationships of accountability with the people they lead. Making themselves accountable in that relationship, employees move to a more satisfying work and personal life.

Group meetings where there are exhortations to do important things and an annual performance review will not establish accountability. There is a place for those things, but taken alone, they will never produce the needed results.

Most managers admit that their experience of annual performance reviews is that they do not produce much improvement in performance. Like everything else, they can be done poorly or well. Great managers learn how to use them well.

Exhortation, well done, can call out energy and even inspire a group with its significance—the meaning and value of its contribution to the culture. Exhortation has its place. Inspiration is valuable. Managers manage shared meanings. They affirm values. But, by itself, exhortation is not a strategy for management over time.

Using the lever of accountability well means planning for multiple interventions that can be understood separately, but must be coordinated.

BUILD ASYMMETRICAL COLLABORATIVE POWER RELATIONSHIPS

Management is an asymmetrical collaborative power relationship. As a working relationship, rather than a personal relationship, it is not a relationship among equals. If that statement troubles you, perhaps you can think of yourself as first among equals—equal in humanity. Managers take up the responsibility to see the larger picture more clearly, carry the responsibility for organizational success more fully, make decisions that have a larger impact on the whole organization, risk the greater potential damage that their mistakes can cause and support and enlarge the contributions of subordinates.

Building an asymmetrical collaborative power relationship starts with a manager taking a risk. The manager affirms that she is there for the subordinate—ready, willing and able to help the subordinate succeed. This is a supportive affirmation of the manager's power. A manager probably will not use that exact phrase, but the message comes across— or doesn't.

Taking this step is a risk because the subordinate may not receive your offer, may feel that it comes out of an enlarged ego rather than a genuine desire to serve or may distort your message in any of a hundred and one ways. But managers are expected to, and are paid to, take the risk.

Offering yourself as a resource is the minimum foundation for accountability. People will not hold themselves accountable in a relationship with a manager who does not affirm his readiness to help.

The relationship is not only one of asymmetrical power. It is also collaborative. Great managers make room for the power of subordinates to stand alongside their own. It is as though they are saying, "Come, drawing on your strengths and mine, let's see what we can accomplish together." Collaboration allows subordinates to hold themselves accountable, which is the only accountability that really works.

Collaboration also means that the relationship is founded on joint accountability. Great managers make themselves accountable to their subordinates. It is one foundation of trust. Make commitments and keep them or renegotiate. If you find that you can't keep a commitment you have made, don't pretend it didn't happen and hope they won't notice. They will. Tell them, tell them why, and renegotiate. You will not lose trust; you will gain it. And you will find that they will be more likely to make themselves accountable to you.

INSPIRE A GROUP WITH THE MEANING AND VALUE OF ITS WORK

During training at a national poultry processing company one day, a group of managers said that it was hard to challenge their subordinates to excel, "Because all we do is kill chickens." I asked them what it would be like for them to tell people that what they really do is make it possible for people of modest means, even poor people, to eat well because they can buy a chicken for under $3.00 and have a great dinner. It was like a comic strip where you see a light bulb go on over the head of someone who is seeing something old in a new way. Light bulbs went on all over the room. The managers saw the meaning of work in a different light. Great managers do this for a group.

Call it reframing. Managers set reality in a different frame, and the picture looks different. Is it killing chickens, or is it providing a valuable resource to the culture? It's both. But which frame you put it in becomes a powerful influence on how people see their work. Framing establishes meaning. And when people see their work as significant and valuable, they are far more likely to hold themselves accountable for doing it well.

DELEGATE

Effective delegation gets the work done and also develops the capacities of subordinates. Still, some managers make only minimal use of delegation. On the surface, this is hard to understand because it seems obvious that delegating increases the productivity of a group and frees a manager for other work. Understanding must be sought beneath the surface.

Delegating can feel like a loss of control. It's the feeling that "I can do it better myself and if I do it, I know it will get done." A manager cannot delegate ultimate accountability for the results her unit achieves. Even after a delegation, the buck still stops with the manager. She delegates tasks and projects but, while holding the person delegated accountable, continues to carry ultimate accountability. This is the source of the anxiety about loss of control. The decision to delegate is a decision to risk sharing managerial accountability. Be brave. Take prudent risks for greater performance by your unit and the development of subordinates.

A manager may feel that delegating and following up may take more time than just doing the work himself. He says, "I delegated it to him, but I had to check back all the time to make sure it was getting done. I could have done it myself in half the time." This is a signal that the manager has either delegated something beyond the abilities of the subordinate, delegated poorly or monitors too closely. These things rob the development potential in delegation.

Ineffective delegation may require excessive time to supervise, evaluate, correct and arbitrate disagreements that arise among employees. The employee who has received the delegation may find himself in a difficult place because of lack of know-how, experience or information. Stress levels and interpersonal conflict may increase when tasks, resources, authority and accountability are unclear.

The first question is when to delegate. How do managers decide?

There are some times when a manager should not delegate. Delegating a task because you are busy and don't want to be bothered with it is one of those times. If you only delegate when you are overloaded, employees will know that and feel discounted.

Delegating as a way of loading up an employee who has been coasting can be a way of avoiding a needed discussion of your concern with the employee. Delegating as a substitute for confronting poor performance sends a mixed message and invites more poor performance.

There are many good reasons to delegate:

- Delegating demonstrates trust and confidence in employees
- It helps prepare employees who have management potential
- Subordinates might have skills in areas where you do not
- It increases your discretionary time for the tasks that only you can do
- It builds productivity

Delegation becomes ineffective when critical elements of delegation are omitted and when the manager who is delegating neglects follow-up and accountability.

An effective delegation clarifies four things:

1. Task
2. Authority
3. Resources
4. Accountability

Task

What is to be done and when is it to be accomplished? Delegate for results, not activities. Tell the subordinate what it should look like when the task is finished. How will things be different than they are now? There are two reasons for this. First, the nature of work is such that you can have an awful lot of activity without achieving much. Second, you want to make sure the person you are delegating to understands the end result that is needed while leaving much of how they are to go about it up to them.

At the conclusion of the delegation, don't ask, "Do you understand?" It is tempting for some employees to say that they do rather than admit that they don't. Also, a "yes" answer ends the dialogue. Instead, ask, "How do you think you will want to go about this? What will you do first?" Their answer will let you know whether they understand and also start their thinking and planning.

Authority

What is the extent of the authority the subordinate will have? What are the limits of their authority? Are there any sacred cows that they should not offend? Are they at liberty to request the help of other employees?

Specify the level of initiative you expect. What freedom of independent action are they to have and what periodic reporting to you? You decide this before the delegation conference based on the subordinate's skills and judgment.

- "When it's finished, let's talk. I'll be interested."

- "If you need to see me as you work on this, let me know."

- "Let's get together for a few minutes every other Friday until you finish this."

- "Check with me first before any decisions or turns in the road. Keep me informed."

Resources

- Time—Are you carving out some of the subordinate's usual responsibilities to make time for the delegation?

- Money—Will the task require expenditures? How much?

- Help—Will your subordinate have help from peers in the unit? If so, you will want to communicate this to the peers.

Accountability

What criteria will you be using to evaluate the successful completion of the delegation? Some delegations will be evaluated based on all of the traditional markers, others on less.

- Quality—And how will that be measured?

- Quantity—How many?

- Timeliness—Was the work completed on time?

- Cost—Did the person stay within the budget?

As you discuss the delegation together, be clear about what is to be accomplished and why. Show the connection between the work and the organization's priorities. Describe the benefit to the personal interests, aspirations and development goals of the subordinate. A good delegation is a conversation, not a directive. You want the subordinate to participate in ways that facilitate their making it their own. Once you have delegated, avoid closely monitoring the way in which subordinates accomplish tasks. Excessive supervision destroys empowerment.

Avoid reverse delegation. Once you have delegated, beware of allowing yourself to be manipulated into relieving the subordinate of the responsibility for decisions and actions. This can happen in the blink of an eye. The employee encounters you in the hall and says, "We've got a problem with that project." When this happens, managers making good use of delegation decide how to structure their availability and participation.

If you tell the employee what to do or suggest that you will need to think it through before deciding, the responsibility for the next move becomes yours. Reverse delegation is complete. It is critically important for the employee's development that responsibility for the next move be theirs. One way to ensure this is to ask the employee to reflect on his choices and come to see you later to discuss what they have decided and why.

Make delegation a routine part of your management—not a safety valve to use only when you get overburdened. Effective delegation will build the performance capacity of your unit and develop employees.

BUILD AN ARCHITECTURE FOR ACCOUNTABILITY

Accountability can only be exercised in a clear and compelling structure for work and relationships. Call it an architecture. There are seven pillars that managers put in place.

1. Alignment between the Wildly Important Priorities and daily work

2. Key measures of successful performance

3. Negotiated commitments

4. A scoreboard

5. Analysis of the data to get to the knowledge

6. Coaching

7. Performance reviews

Great managers understand that these are not seven separate good ideas. They do not jump from implementing one to trying another—"Let's try a scoreboard!" The seven are organically related and achieve their leverage by being integrated into a single system of managing for accountability. They are the architecture in which a manager does his work.

1. **Alignment between the Wildly Important Priorities and daily work.** Far too frequently, organizations describe high-minded missions, write ambitious vision statements, list goals and objectives and talk about Wildly Important Priorities without helping people be clear with each other about what these things lead to behaviorally. This leaves people disillusioned and wondering what all the work to define objectives was about. Effective managers help people understand what they are to do in order to execute on the Wildly Important Priorities. Without this alignment between priorities and defined actions, the espoused priorities remain noble ideas that don't have much impact.

   Building alignment enlists managers and employees in conversations that lead to consensus statements like these:

   • It is a priority with us to deliver world-class customer service; therefore, every sales and delivery person will conduct a customer satisfaction survey with all their customers three times a year and submit a report summarizing and analyzing the findings and laying plans for improvement.

- We value [XYZ]; therefore, we _____.
- It is our strategy to [ABC]; therefore, we will _____.

The value of these efforts is found in the connections that they build. Work activities disconnected from values and priorities become soul-draining drudgery. Values and priorities disconnected from the activities of day-to-day work become platitudes that breed cynicism. Managers ensure against these dangers. They build connecting bridges between the values employees hold and what they are doing on the job. They span the gap between principles and performance. And they talk about these connections—all the time!

2. **Key measures of successful performance.** Managers decide, with their employees, what are the key measures of organization, unit and personal success.

Not everything that counts can be counted. Some of the most important things are hard to quantify: fair and equitable treatment of employees, prudent risk-taking that supports new ventures, transparent communication, balanced concern for the interests of all stakeholders (customers, employees, stockholders, executives and board members, suppliers). These things arise from the spirit of an organization and its leaders and cannot be measured except as they contribute, in a global way, to long-term well being and prosperity.

However, identifying a few key measures of efficient and effective operation assists managers to hold people accountable and avoid happy-talk not supported by the facts.

Measures also help a manager avoid subjectivity in evaluating the performance of individuals. This becomes particularly important during formal, documented performance reviews.

Some managers and employees fear that spirit will be lost when figures are used to control operations. There is a common experience in neighborhood life that helps put this fear to rest. On a Saturday morning, a group of guys are horsing around shooting baskets on the school outdoor basketball court. Someone says, "Hey, let's choose up sides and keep score." What happens to the quality of play? What happens to the spirit and energy of the group? You know. You are looking to identify a few key measures. Not too many. Too many, and you get buried under statistical reports. Too many, and people get lost in the data before they have opportunity to ask what the data is saying. You may want to ask your group something like this, "How could we know if we are really doing an excellent job here? What are two, three, no more than five key measures of success?"

They might be surprised at being asked. You might be surprised at the insight revealed in their answers. All of you might enjoy, and profit from, the discussion.

3. **Negotiated commitments.** Once it is determined what key measures will be used, managers face the task of getting commitment to execute on them. Requirements can be announced; commitment must be negotiated. If a manager does not have the luxury of negotiating—if requirements are announced by a more senior level of management—the middle manager still negotiates for ownership of the requirements by subordinates.

This explains one reason why it is called "middle management." Middle managers represent top leadership to the front line and represent the front line to top leadership. They literally are in the middle—between a rock and a hard place.

In this situation, a manager talks with subordinates, individually or as a group, touching every base. She:

- Explains the meaning and importance of the required execution on the key measures

- Links the measures to the vision of a preferred and possible future

- Defines her contribution to assisting people to attain the objectives

- Expresses confidence that the group will achieve

- Conveys her expectation of best effort and expresses the hope that everyone can commit themselves

- Asks for an expression of commitment. "Wayne, I hope I can count on your for this. We need your contribution. Are you on board?"

The sequence of actions here is not an outline for a speech. All of this takes place in what could reasonably be called "the miracle of dialogue." The miracle happens when a manager uses the voice of confident leadership to affirm rather than defend and indicates flexibility of means if not of desired ends.

4. **A scoreboard.** Given key measures and commitments, you need a scoreboard that can be viewed 24/7 and reveals individual and group contributions.

The scoreboard, like the key measures, must be the tool of your employees for self direction, not a tool to be used by management to manipulate them. Identify the key measures and build the scoreboard with your direct reports, not for them. Of course, a manager has veto power over deciding what is most important, but great managers involve their direct reports in ways that make use of the veto power infrequent. You may be surprised that employees will place the standard higher than you would.

When it's the bottom of the ninth inning and your team is behind one run, there's a man on second base, and a 300 hitter stands in the batters box, do you think his awareness of the score and the situation makes a difference? You know it does. Baseball, a game obsessed with statistics, can even tell you what a given batter's average is when there are men on base in scoring position. Almost always it is higher than their overall average. Something important is at stake. The scoreboard shows it.

Life is like that. Organizational life is not an exception.

Some managers will fear that showing the score of individuals on the scoreboard will create competition leading to bad feelings and lower morale. Try telling that to the manager of the baseball team that won the World Series last year. Every player can see exactly what everyone's batting average, fielding percentage or earned run average was at any time during the year. Yet the team cohesion of winners is extraordinary.

A working unit in a business organization is not a baseball team, but it is a team. When a manager expects team members to support and encourage each other's performance rather than criticize it, the scoreboard becomes a call to team excellence. When a manager uses the scoreboard to coach rather than referee, it soon becomes clear to subordinates that the facts are friendly. Attitude is everything.

You need a scoreboard that makes the situation so clear that no one can miss being aware of reality. Create a compelling scoreboard. Place it where everyone can see it, any time. Hold everyone accountable—all the time.

5. **Analysis of the data to get to the knowledge.** Managers believe and communicate the belief to their group that the facts are friendly. But what a friend is saying often needs interpretation. Reports on the key measures are just data. A manager, overburdened with too many reports, too many key measures, a data deluge, expressed a common longing, "Where is the knowledge born out of the data, and where is the wisdom born out of the knowledge?"

Data itself has no meaning. Meanings are supplied by people who look to the data for understanding of what it reveals. Perception determines meanings. Smart, well intentioned people can look at the same data and perceive different meanings. Perception is not objective. An individual's perception is rooted in his history—he expects to see what he has seen before. It is rooted in his assumptions. He assumes that because unit X has the kind of people he judges them to be that their data will confirm his prejudices. Perception is rooted in what the individual is capable of perceiving based on his experience, knowledge and capacity for insight.

Even more challenging, the knowledge derived from perceiving the data does not clearly reveal what to do about it. That is a matter for judgment. At a certain period in the early 20th century, a manager observing that the sale of buggy whips was declining might conclude that the salesmen needed an incentive plan, or that a new design was needed.

When data reveals a shortfall on a given key measure of operational success, astute managers will stay open to a variety of interpretations until dialogue with a more senior manager, peers and subordinates can clarify what the data is saying. The problem may lie in structures or systems rather than in individuals. When managers suspect this, they ask themselves questions:

- Is the key measure the right one?

- Does it set expectations realistically?

- Is the process of gathering and recording data reliable?

- Are there adequate resources to support performance?

- Can the task be simplified?

- Is there more shortfall in unit X than in unit Y, and if so, what might explain it other than the capacity of particular individuals?

- Are there other structural or process factors that impede performance?

Of course, the explanation for a shortfall on a key measure may reside closer to the individual than to organizational realities. If this appears to be the case, a manager will ask another group of questions:

- Is the meaning and value of the key measure evident to those who must perform?

- Has there been adequate training and follow-up coaching to support performance?

- Are performers adjusting to new technology, skill sets or expectations that do not easily mesh with the historic identity and values of the organization?

- Are expectations clear and compelling?

- Could he do it if he had to, or is there a gross lack of knowledge or skill?

- Does he have the potential to change?

- What is the consequence of adequate or inadequate performance?

Coaching a manager one day, he complained to me that he could not get his team to perform a task that he saw as important. They didn't do it, or they didn't do it in the right way, or they didn't do it on time.

I asked him, "Why should they do it?" He explained that they should do it because it was important. I said that it was clear that it was important to him, but asked why it should be important to them. He explained that it should be important to them because, "It is just so obvious that it is the right thing to do." I asked what happened when they didn't do it, and what would happen if they did. There was a long silence. It became clear that the manager was carrying the consequences of their nonperformance in his personal frustration and anger, but there was no consequence to his subordinates.

Worse yet is the situation in which there are positive consequences for nonperformance—the expectations get lowered. Or a situation where there are negative consequences for adequate performance—an individual incurs the displeasure of peers for raising the bar. These behaviors are symptoms of an uninvolved or passive manager. Managers cannot afford to let these dynamics continue to have influence. If managers don't reinforce standards with consequences, employees have every right to conclude that the standards do not matter and that consequences will not arise.

What consequences a subordinate predicts, on the basis of past experience with a manager, have a powerful influence on performance. Employees observe, study and draw conclusions about a manager's behavior, just as a manager does about theirs.

6. **Coaching.** In a group of any size, you will be able to distinguish four sub-groups of employees:

- The stars

- The adequate

- The marginal

- The toxic

The stars are hard to find. In fact, you generally don't find them. You develop them. When you have them, you want to do everything you can to retain them. Acknowledge their contribution. Reward it. Make it evident to your team that what the stars are doing is what you are looking for. Yes, play favorites. As long as you play favorites in ways that make it evident that your appreciations and rewards are based on accomplishments and that you are committed to helping others achieve, it's OK. It's better than OK; it applies additional force on your accountability lever.

The adequate are the backbone of your unit. Don't discount them because they are not stars. A few of them can become stars, but no organization can function without managerial support for adequate performers. Let them know that you appreciate them and are committed to helping them develop their capacities and their contribution.

The marginal are those who puzzle you. Can they do better? Are they unwilling or unable? Is there something you can do that you have not tried yet? Should you terminate them? What are they costing you in terms of group morale and energy? Can you muster your nerve to be candid with them?

The toxic must go. You can never take a group to the level of performance your organization needs if you allow people who are toxic to the group to continue poisoning the well. What a person who poisons the well never seems to realize is that they drink from the same well as everyone else. Their behavior is toxic to themselves as well as to others. If, to no avail, you have made diligent efforts to confront and coach, you will have the unpleasant task of calling that to their attention and separating them from employment.

If you do not, if you allow them to continue their toxic influence, some of the marginal people will wonder why they are trying when you tolerate toxic behavior, some of the adequate will become marginal, you will lose the respect of some of the stars, and they will leave. You can't afford to avoid the unpleasant task of confronting the toxic and the pleasant opportunity to coach the other groups for improvement.

The manager who wonders, "Why is coaching needed? Why can't people just do right and be happy?" is in trouble. Human nature is such that we respond to appreciation. We respond to challenge. We want to contribute and respond to people who can show us how. We want to see what capacities are in us and learn to use them well. We want to feel influential and respond to managers who listen to us and show us how to be a positive influence among our peers. We want and need to know when we need to improve our performance.

Coach, don't referee. The difference is important. A referee catches players doing something wrong and penalizes them. A coach spots a player's strengths, shows the way to use them more effectively, spots the weaknesses and shows how to keep them from compromising the strengths, teaches, mentors and helps the player see the possibilities in a different kind of future.

Coaching is the way out of the dead-end "command and control" style. In command and control, a manager decides what must be done and how, tells people to do it and referees their performance.

One of the costs of the command and control style is that it pushes a manager into managing the problems to the exclusion of exploiting the opportunities. There are always problems and less than desirable performance. But if a manager lets the imperative to do things right evolve into an almost exclusive focus on fixing it when things are done wrong, performance will never rise above the level of just barely good enough. "Do no wrong" is not a rallying cry that will call out the team's best contribution. In the environment that is created, people become cautious, play it safe and never excel. You can require people to come to work on time and observe the policies and work rules. You can't require them to bring their passion and energy with them. Good coaching yields self-empowerment. People bring their passion and energy.

Watch for brief, informal coaching opportunities at an employee's worksite, not just those where you have the opportunity to sit down for a scheduled coaching session. Show that you stand ready to help them deal with a new challenge, get something right the first time, learn to manage their time, learn to plan their week to execute on the Wildly Important Priorities, learn how to finish a day's work rather than letting things back up across a week. Coaches don't wait to be asked. Nor do they wait for serious problems to emerge.

This may require more time up front, but you will spend less time solving problems, putting out fires, mopping up spilled milk and refereeing. My mechanic has a sign on his tool chest that says, "If you think you don't have the time to do it right, think how much time it will take to do it over." Funny where you find wisdom about managing.

Managers who are proactive coaches know their employees well enough to understand their strengths and weaknesses and how to challenge them with new assignments. They ask an employee how she intends to handle the task and then discuss the plan. They observe and track performance to identify areas in which employees may need assistance.

Catch an employee doing something right and tell them about it. Pass out praise in public and criticism in private. Empower your praise of your direct reports. You don't just say, "Good job, Johnny." You say, "Good job, Johnny, because what you did made a difference on that Wildly Important Priority you hear me talk about all the time. If that situation ever comes up again, I hope you will do exactly the same thing."

There is a mistaken attribution of conflict between what is called "hard management" and "soft management." Managers who pride themselves in practicing hard management say that what they want, and intend to get, is performance. Performance first. How people feel about it can wait or be dealt with later. But one of the most important ingredients in getting performance is the manager's attitude. So, is the manager who understands that people perform better when they are coached rather than controlled practicing hard or soft management?

Neither. A manager who is a skillful coach has found a third way—not simply hard or soft. Call it empowerment *with* direction. A coaching manager gives up the illusion of control in order to have better control of outcomes.

The question is no longer, "Which is better, hard or soft management?" The question becomes, "How can I best integrate the hard clear focus on the necessity of performance results with the kind of motivational environment that will cause people to work hard because they want to?"

If all you've got is the requirement for hard results, all you get is compliance—not excellence, not going the second mile, not outcomes above and beyond the necessary minimum.

If all you've got is warm fuzzy feelings, all you get is compliance—not excellence, not going the second mile, not outcomes above and beyond the necessary minimum.

The same thing!

When a costly mistake is made or a target goal missed by a group, don't look around for someone to blame. Call mistakes learning opportunities. Call your group together and say something like this, "Well, we blew it this time gang. What can we learn from this? If we had it to do all over again, what would you want to do differently?"

Great coaching blends a tough-minded call for performance with an invitation to robust participation and dialogue from direct reports. Great managers use an astonishing blend of direction and invitation to self-empowerment.

Coaching is not just telling. There is a platform on which the coaching process rests. Managers build this platform. If the platform has not been built well, coaching cannot proceed with integrity. The platform makes it possible for those who can and will to perform. Managers inspect for the adequacy of the platform by asking themselves questions:

- How aware am I of the aspirations, goals and priorities of this individual? What does he want? What motivates him?

  A manager cannot provide effective coaching without this. If you have little understanding of these things, your suggestions in the coaching dialogue will be received like the gift of a suit that doesn't fit.

- Have I effectively communicated what the Wildly Important Priorities (WIPs) are? If I asked her, could she tell me?

- What does this person probably need help with?

- Am I ready for joint accountability? Am I comfortable with the idea that this person should hold me accountable for things in our working relationship?

After these questions for herself, a manager reflects on what questions to use to launch creative give and take in a coaching conversation. Here are some that have been found useful. You may want to use some of them and add your own. Having a framework for the coaching process, shaped around five to ten questions, will help you give direction to the process:

1. Have I made clear where we're going?

2. What are your thoughts about our Wildly Important Priorities?

3. On your best day, how is your work related to those priorities? What does it look like? What's happening? What are you doing?

4. On a scale of 1 – 10 (10 being all the time), how often is that happening now?

5. What do you see as barriers to your success? What are two or three things that could be done that would help you move your answer to my previous question up a number? How can I help you increase your focus?

6. What are you proud of in your work recently?

7. It has been my experience that _____. I wonder, do you think that approach could help you?

8. What are two or three things that are contributing to your success in this job?

9. What do you need from me?

10. Do you have some suggestions for me?

How often to coach? In every conversation. These questions are not only to be used in a formal coaching interview. Effective managers bring some version of at least one or two of them to every conversation they have with subordinates.

Depending on the number of people in your unit and the time available, you might provide a formal, sit-down coaching session four to twelve times a year or more as needed.

7. **Performance reviews.** Organizations have requirements for a periodic, often annual, formal, documented review of the performance of employees. They are often the basis for decisions about compensation and promotion. Employees dread the surprises that might come or look forward to the salary increase they might receive. Managers usually don't believe they have much effect on performance—and they usually don't. There is an almost universal feeling that they have become a meaningless exercise.

The problem here is not unique, and it is not puzzling. Any intervention by management that is not integrated with others and not supported by a coherent philosophy of management becomes problematic. At best, it becomes "the flavor of the month" that employees understand will have no more effect than the last flavor did. At worst, it breeds cynicism.

If formal performance reviews are to be rescued, managers must:

- Integrate them with prior coaching

- Involve the employee in shaping them

- Use them to negotiate new performance commitments

- Include a development plan

- Hold employees accountable going forward

The amazing thing is that so often managers will agree with these principles and proceed to disregard them. The press of today's problems, the urgency to produce results without taking too much time to lay the foundation for achieving results and multiple distractions conspire to distract managers from the leverage a performance review contains. The leverage becomes hard to see through the fog. Performance reviews continue to look like a distraction from work rather than a support of it. Too often laying the foundations for performance is what is done when there is time left over, and there is never time left over.

It is a sad truth that the natural drift in organizational life is not toward excellence. The natural drift in organizations, if nature takes its course, is toward undesirable ends, fragmented effort, disconnected priorities and declining performance. This is not terribly surprising when you understand that it's the same way in all of creation. The natural drift of an untended garden is toward weeds and under-production. The natural drift of the human body, if not cared for, is toward premature aging and illness. The natural drift of a home, if not maintained, is toward disrepair and reduced value. Managers understand this trend in organizational life and that they are commissioned to turn it around—to tend the garden, care for the organizational body and leverage human effort.

Stephen R. Covey wrote an excellent one-page article, "Beyond the Performance Review," in which he suggests that performance reviews be built on previously negotiated "win-win agreements" in which managers:

> "… seek to deeply and accurately understand the 'wins' for their employees … sit down with their employees and make 'win-win agreements.' The employee defines what the win is for him or her, and the leader defines what the win is for the organization … First, you define together the goal of the agreement—the desired results. Then you define, again together, the guidelines, resources and accountability mechanisms you will use—that is, how and when you will account for progress on the goal. Finally, you define the wins for both of you if you achieve the goal—and the consequences if you don't."

This simultaneously makes the annual performance review easier, lowers the anxiety that usually surrounds it and increases its power to leverage performance.

Good periodic coaching leads to a "no surprises" annual performance review. If an employee leaves an annual performance review conference surprised with negative feedback, it's a clear sign that coaching during the year was not well done.

The manager who has brief notes on each coaching session is well prepared to write an annual review. Some managers have employees sign their notes indicating that they have read them with the manager. Some managers also ask employees to document their understanding of each coaching session and what they plan to do in response to its challenges. The manager simply says something like this:

> "Ann, please send me a memo by Friday summarizing our discussion together today and saying what you're going to do about the plans and suggestions we considered. No more than two or three paragraphs. If you take more than fifteen minutes to write this, you're working too hard. This will help keep both of us on track going forward."

You could also keep a performance diary. Ease and simplicity are the keys to making it have value for you. You keep a locked file on each employee you coach. When the employee does something really good, or really deficient, you take out the file, get a pencil and write two or three sentences. No form to fill out. Don't make this laborious or you won't do it. Again, it contributes to making writing your annual review easier and keeps you from being biased by the last wonderful or awful thing the employee did.

A good many managers have the employee who is to be reviewed write their own draft of a review before the conference. Some have the employee use the same form that the manager must finally document. Others ask the employee to write them a letter summarizing their performance over the year, including:

- Strong positive results

- Challenges that were not met as well as they might have been

- Recommendations for their development plan

- Commitments going forward

The virtue of all of these possibilities is that they involve the employee as a participant in the review rather than only being its recipient. A good review is not a pronouncement from on high. It is a collaboration. The manager has the final responsibility for documenting the review, but when the employee has participated in its shaping, it has far greater leverage.

Action Steps You Can Take

If you want to empower yourself in the use of the accountability lever, here are some things you can think through and do.

- Think this through—between unstructured permissiveness and behaviors that your direct reports would describe as over-controlling, which is the greater potential trap for you? How effective are you being in charting the middle course of coaching described here?

- Are there ways you want to re-frame the mission and work of your unit to make its meaning and value more obvious? If so, write down what you might want to say.

- Rate yourself on the effectiveness of your delegations on a scale of 1 – 10 with 10 being the best. Make some notes describing how you plan to make it more effective.

- How can you build a better, more obvious bridge between the Wildly Important Priorities and what people are to do every week to support them? Make some notes.

- Write down one key measure that you are unwilling to compromise and describe how you will engage your group in dialogue and negotiation

- Build a scoreboard—computerized, flip chart or black/whiteboard

- Make a list of ten positive and ten negative consequences that you can use to enhance a subordinate's performance

- Think through how you can use the 10-question coaching process described on pages 105 – 106.

- Make a list of changes you will make in the way you use the annual performance review

The 6th Lever: Alignment

"Individual commitment to a group effort—that is what makes a team work, a company work, a society work, a civilization work!"

—Vince Lombardi

Vince Lombardi, one of the most successful coaches in the history of American football, understood the power of a team in which everyone is aligned. Alignment makes things work: football teams, companies, societies and civilizations. Team members more committed to the group effort (winning the game) than to their own stardom make the team work for everyone. Is everyone running the same play? Toward the same goal line? With the same passion? When they are, things work. Coaches and managers point the way. They use the leveraging power of alignment.

Alignment is everybody pulling on the same rope in the same direction. It is every department of an organization in full collaboration with every other department so that turf guarding is changed into common turf infused with spirit. It is a clear line of sight between the strategic plan and what is happening every day—how people spend their time, how they focus and execute the plan.

Alignment is foundational for successful organizations. When you have it, it feels like: 1 + 1 = 3

The effort of one division, department, team or individual leverages that of another. The total is more than the sum of the parts. This is the reason we have organizations—they multiply individual effort. When it is not happening, working feels like you are trying to open an umbrella in a Volkswagen.

People know when their organization isn't aligned. You can hear it in their talk. Robert Reich, U.S. Secretary of Labor in the Clinton Administration, listens using what he calls the pronoun test. The test works like this: You ask people to tell you about their place of work—to tell you what they do and what it's like to work where they work. Then you don't listen as much to the content of their answer as you listen for the pronouns they use. If they use the pronoun "they," if they tell you what "they" are doing, the organization flunks the pronoun test for alignment. If they use "we" and "our," you know that it's a workplace that has cultivated alignment. You know that employees feel that their work is aligned with the organization's goals.

Great managers build alignment. They talk about it. They call people to it. They celebrate it when it is born. Why? Not just because it is a worthy principle, but because it is the foundation of organizational power—the power to ensure survival, excellence and lasting contribution.

When there is total alignment in an organization, everything lines up in the service of the goals and objectives. There is coherence of intent and effort among:

Values and Vision
Goals and Objectives
Strategy
Priorities
Policy
Structure
Processes
Incentives
Resources
Divisions and Departments
Teams
Levels of Management
Individual Employees
Daily Work

The end result? Results. Period.

The truth of this is so obvious and managers are so accustomed to seeing these words used to describe an organization that this call to action washes over consciousness without sticking. The list, and more importantly the alignment among items, shows what defines an organization and holds it together.

Without alignment it feels like the wheels are coming off. The tone is like that in a family when one partner wants to spend the savings on education and preparation for a better career and the other wants to spend it on a great vacation.

When the allocation of resources is not aligned with the stated values, cynicism results. People stop believing the leaders. When the proclaimed strategy is not reflected in the structures, confusion and anxiety reign. The symptoms of misalignment are well known:

- Managers say that they value employees as the greatest asset and that they want every brain in the game, but employees feel that they are not listened to

- The top leaders of the organization say that one key strategy is to compete effectively in the changing marketplace, but they cut the training and research budgets

- Department X says that its mission is to support the work and contribute to the success of other departments, but repeatedly blames Department Y for failures

- Front-line employees say that "the mission is everything," but put personal agendas and preferences first

- Teams find that they are discussing the same concerns and making the same decisions month after month, but things are not changing. Execution is not aligning with decisions.

- Supervisors push for measurable quality, but quality is not incentivized by the compensation system

Managers take it as their responsibility to identify these and scores of other symptoms of misalignment and to intervene.

ALIGN WITH YOUR MANAGER

The alignment over which you have most influence is your alignment with your manager and his interpretation of the goals of the organization and the objectives of your unit. This is important because some of your ability to lead your group depends on the clarity, transparency and trust in the relationship you have with your manager. You need your manager's backing, and you need to feel in sync with the direction of the organization if you are to bring your best contribution.

When you leave a meeting with your group and sit with your manager, the tables have been turned. You are the authority for your group. Your manager is the authority for you.

Skillful management of this shift will draw the respect of your manager and make it more likely that you will receive his backing. Here are some guidelines that will help:

- *Position yourself as a collaborator toward shared objectives.* Avoid a demanding or overly deferential manner. Demonstrate your knowledge and acceptance of company goals and strategy. Show that you have clear ideas about how these mesh with the work of your unit or team.

- *Think like a manager.* When you request additional resources, make it clear that you have thought through the cost/benefit ratio inherent in your request. Is it a request that will enhance revenue, raise costs or have a neutral effect on revenue?

- *Realize that your manager is just about as human as you are.* She will make mistakes, make decisions you will not agree with and not always anticipate every twist and turn in the road ahead. Don't kid yourself with the false belief that a manager at a superior level in an organization should be above these shortcomings.

- *Make your peace with the reality that your manager is permitted to direct you to do things that you may not be thrilled about.* Your manager carries responsibilities and risks that are larger than yours. You are equals in your humanity but not in your roles and responsibilities. Don't confuse the two.

  Mark Twain described his relationship with an argumentative river boat pilot he worked under, "He did his arguing with heat ... and I did mine with the reserve and moderation of a subordinate who does not like to be flung out of a pilot-house that is perched forty feet above the water."

- *Don't waste your political capital on trivial issues and concerns.* Save your strongest affirmations for those things that will have the largest impact on business results. Only be absolute when ethics or integrity are at stake.

- *Support the decisions of your manager and the management team you are a member of.* When you become a manager, your primary loyalty is to them. Your second loyalty is to the group you lead. This is a hard saying for some managers. Having risen from the ranks, new managers often feel more loyalty to the front line than to their new responsibilities. But managers are expected to work on behalf of the whole organization and participate in and support decisions that affect the whole—even when they may appear to disadvantage the unit they lead.

ALIGNMENT BETWEEN ORGANIZATIONAL UNITS

Early in my career in management, the manager of another department and I had a disagreement that was chronic and getting worse. It was compromising our efficiency. It was beginning to affect our subordinates. Finally, the CEO called us both in and said something like this:

> "Gentlemen, the conflict between you has gone on for far too long. It is to the point that it has become self-sustaining so that it hardly matters what you are arguing about—the argument, not the subject, has become the main thing. It's personal. This is beginning to affect the effectiveness of the units each of you manage. We have important work to do. Our goal is ambitious. I cannot, and I will not, allow your personal disagreements to compromise our ability to achieve that goal. So, if the two of you don't resolve this, I'm going to have to decide which one of you I can do without."

We resolved it.

There is a tendency for units within an organization to nurture too much separateness from other units. When this happens, their managers can easily feel more loyalty to their unit than to the well-being of the whole. Accountability only flows upward within the unit rather than also laterally to peer managers. Competition rather than collaboration can begin to rule.

This kind of unit has been referred to as a smokestack. All accountability flows up the smokestack. There is insulation from related processes in other units. Lateral collaboration suffers. This is a classic example of an unaligned organization. Units are focused too much on their own operation and success and not enough aligned with the higher good— organizational success.

Managers in the smokestacks have limited influence in changing this. The drive for change must come from above—a more senior manager. Middle managers often start the change process by calling the cost of the smokestacks to the attention of senior leaders. There is a principle here—what you can't change, you describe. Your ability to influence and persuade resides in your ability to describe the cost with such clarity that a more senior leader will share your concern. If initial efforts fail, remind yourself that it is your responsibility to persuade, not your manager's responsibility to become persuaded.

The cost of smokestack dynamics in an organization is reflected in duplication of effort, blocking or slowing of processes that must involve more than one unit, secret-keeping that breeds ill feeling and reduced revenue.

A public service organization I worked with was having difficulty billing accurately for their services. There was constant irritation between the service providers and the business office. Each blamed the other for problems variously characterized as inadequate reporting, data entry error, late reporting and poor attitudes. This had gone on for months and was very expensive. Rather than doing it right the first time, work had to be repeated. Invoices were late getting out, which slowed cash flow and increased nonpayment. Training and retraining hadn't helped. Shaming people hadn't helped.

Finally a leader said, "Let's put the business office staff who handle these reporting functions in the service sites. Let's relocate their offices." Skillful managers at various sites used this change to, in various ways, recast relationships, teams, understandings and work flow at their sites. But it was the voice of leadership, challenging how things had always been structured, that opened up a whole new approach to operational efficiency. Structural change, dismantling smokestacks, produced process change which increased revenue.

The principle here is cross-function accountability. Accountability no longer only flows upward. Cross-function accountability is established by the manager the various functions and units report to. By interventions to restructure accountability and by modeling the expected behavior, managers break down the smokestacks.

This has a remarkable effect beyond restructuring accountability. It multiplies communication, increases mutual support and generates creativity. The best ideas flow freely from one unit to another. Success stories get around. Best practices in one unit get adopted by others. The structure has been called a "boundaryless organization." Managers facilitate this constant flow. They create structures in which such sharing is the agenda and the motivating force.

Consider these graphical representations of the change from a smokestack model to the boundaryless model in which accountability and communication of best practices flow in multiple streams.

The Smokestack Model

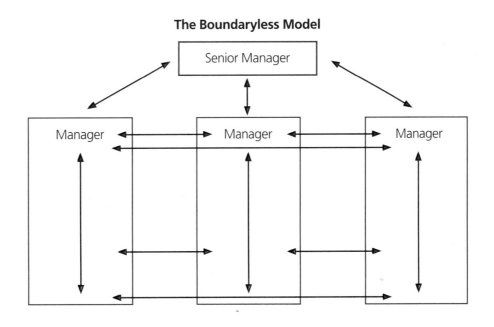

The Boundaryless Model

This paradigm shift can be executed at any level—from the most senior executive group of a large corporation to small teams of a few people reporting to a common supervisor in a given department. The dynamics and benefits are the same. A unit having sub-units, each reporting to managers who are peers with one another, does not automatically align and empower itself for achieving the overarching goals. That begins to happen when the managers expect and model cross-function accountability and boundaryless communication.

As an illustration of implementing these understandings, consider an organization that decides to begin each meeting of the middle management group by asking each manager for a brief report summarizing the priorities they are working on, what is going well, concerns where they are not succeeding as expected, what they are planning to do to address those concerns and what they need from their fellow managers. The leader of the meeting expects the group of peer managers to become peer supervisors holding each other accountable for results and supporting and coaching each other when there are shortfalls.

The lead manager models the working relationship that she expects, thus driving out the fear that self-revelation and joint accountability will become an invitation to criticism or attack.

This change uses the lever of accountability to great effect.

Chain of command

The concept of chain of command comes from the military where it indicates the line of authority along which orders and communication are passed. Subordinates deal with the authority immediately above them. Commanders give orders to those immediately below them. The Private does not report to the General, nor does the General usually command the Private.

Civilian organizations have generally adopted these traditional understandings. A matrix organization blends this traditional formal organization and understanding with the inclusion of project managers. Thus, a given staff member may have relationships of accountability both to their traditional functional department and a project manager. This structure creates synergistic benefits by sharing responsibility between project and traditional functional management.

Whether an organization has traditional functional departments or a matrix model, managers attend to the chain of command dynamics. Their intention is to maximize alignment between individuals and units and to prevent the chaos that results when a chain of command is not respected.

ALIGNMENT WITHIN A WORKING UNIT

Alignment of purpose and execution among the members of a working unit is essential for the achievement of objectives. In its absence, several symptoms appear:

- Decisions are made but not implemented

- Personal agendas undermine group cohesion

- Apparent consensus turns out to be more apparent than real

- When all is said and done, more is said than done

- Conflicts remain unresolved and drain energy

Great managers intervene to treat these symptoms of misalignment. They use several initiatives which, taken together, build alignment in the unit.

The superordinate goal

The superordinate goal is that larger thing that forestalls small things like competition between units, pettiness, distracting personal agendas and secret keeping.

Great managers have a crystal clear understanding of the goal that stands above all others for their unit. They frame their unit's superordinate goal in ways that align it with the superordinate goal of the organization. They frame it in ways that invite an emotional attachment from every member of the team.

At every opportunity they voice this superordinate goal. They become cheerleaders for it. They affirm their belief that everything else must come into alignment with it. They require that it does not get changed or deleted.

Conflict resolution strategies

Conflict is unavoidable. Perspectives on reality are so diverse. Facts can be found to support almost any position. Ego can override rationality. The capacity for conflict appears to be built into human nature and the nature of relationships. This is not good or bad, it just is.

Managers want to use conflict as a tool for surfacing multiple ideas, perspectives and recommendations and feeding all of them into a positive decision-making process. They understand that if this is not done, if conflict is not directed positively toward contribution and eventual resolution, the organization will pay an unacceptable price.

The price is revealed when groups revisit the same decisions over and over again. The price appears in after-the-meeting meetings to voice what could not be voiced in the meeting. The final costly price appears in the loss of the capacity to execute on the priorities. Unresolved conflict, not conflict, is the villain.

Managers garner the benefits of conflict by encouraging robust dialogue and rigorous challenge in meetings. They model it. They express their appreciation when those attending advocate for divergent viewpoints. They invite disagreement, focused on issues not personalities, as the group searches for the best among alternative ways of working. They normalize conflict and affirm its value. In this environment, people can take each other on and express honest disagreement without appearing rude or hostile.

Patrick Lencioni, who has written well on teambuilding, calls this "mining for conflict":

> "Even when norms have been set, most people will shy away from conflict when they aren't accustomed to it. And that's why a team leader must become a miner of conflict. What does that mean? It means the leader must seek out opportunities for unearthing buried conflict and forcing team members to address those issues."

When a leader effectively mines for conflict and then facilitates eventual decision making, people leave the meeting feeling that their contribution has been heard and considered. Even if their divergent viewpoint did not prevail, they feel respected, not discounted. It is precisely this process of robust dialogue around important issues that creates commitment even when 100% consensus was not achieved.

Have you wondered why decisions are made in a meeting and six weeks later nothing has changed? It is the struggle with difficult issues that gets commitment to action and change. Announcement won't get it. Memos won't get it. Slogans won't get it. Commands won't get it. Micromanagement won't get it. Meetings that do not call out divergent perspectives and recommendations, leaving some unspoken, won't get it. Participation in the struggle with voice and choice gets alignment and commitment.

Conflict is helpful, but this is not an invitation to protracted argument, division and chaos. When there is a poorly defined problem, when there is an incomplete set of possible solutions, and when there is little agreement on how to move forward, managers call team members to sharpen definitions and broaden the range of possible directions. When a group suppresses this process, they run the risk of nonperformance around a prematurely made decision. Managers invite disagreement then channel the process toward shared commitment to a shared decision.

Intel Corporation has a saying, "Disagree and commit." Early disagreement is expected, even invited, but then teams are called to unite behind the shared decision.

Managers can help their group get more comfortable in conflictual situations by inviting the group to look together at their style. Individuals have a preference for a certain style of engaging in conflict. Over time, a group will develop a style that it turns to most often when conflict emerges. Some of these styles are more productive than others. By examining their preferred style, and choosing to expand it, groups can increase the likelihood that conflict will be a positive contributor to their work.

The Thomas-Killman Conflict Mode Instrument has been used by working groups for many years to understand and expand their ways of resolving conflict. An Internet search for "Thomas-Killman conflict mode" found 243 references. The instrument identifies five predominant modes that people employ in engaging in conflict:

1. **Competing**—When individuals and groups are in competing mode, people are not cooperating. They are asserting their own positions with a will to win.

2. **Collaborating**—When they are in collaborating mode, people are also being assertive but tempering assertiveness by relating cooperatively. They are attempting to work toward a third alternative to the conflicting positions in which both can experience a win. Resolution of the conflict is found in what many have called a win/win.

3. **Compromising**—Compromising mode also finds people being both assertive and cooperative, but rather than continuing to work to find a win/win, they find an acceptable solution that partially meets the needs of both parties—not as personally satisfying as a win/win.

4. **Avoiding**—People in the avoiding mode are neither asserting nor cooperative. Conflict is simply avoided. It is a strategy involving repressing conflict and delaying dealing with it.

5. **Accommodating**—When individuals or groups are in accommodating mode, they are unassertive and cooperative. This mode is the opposite of competing. The goal here is to yield to the position of another.

From a management perspective, there may be appropriate times for each of the modes, but there are many situations in which the collaboration mode is preferable. When groups collaborate their way through conflict, decisions are made that not only save face for everyone, as in a compromise, but that also result in a better approach than any of the parties had envisioned.

Consulting with the senior management team of a mid-sized organization, I invited them to draft a "Rules of Engagement" document saying how they would work to handle disagreements, resolve conflict and create alignment. I suggested they frame the document around the following outline. You might want to have your unit create a similar document.

RULES OF ENGAGEMENT

1. When our group is making a decision, we want those who disagree with the direction the process is going in to _____ _____

2. When they do so, we will respond by _____ _____

3. When we notice "after the meeting meetings" in which views contrary to decisions made at the meeting are being expressed, we will _____ _____

4. We will create an environment in which it is safe to disagree. We can do this by____ _____

5. We ask our CEO to help us abide by these shared commitments by _____ _____

6. Once decisions have been made by our management group, we will all back those decisions with our units. We will ensure that this is happening by _____ _____

Powerful promises were made. In discussing the seventh point, the group decided that after important decisions were made in a meeting, each of the managers would convey the decision to their group by the end of the following business day. They would then send the CEO a one-paragraph memo (with copies to their peer managers) stating that they had informed their group and summarizing the group's response.

Finally, the group decided to have their Rules of Engagement document laminated and to pass around a copy at each meeting until the understandings and commitments became a routine characteristic of their culture.

Changes like this are borne on the wings of robust dialogue. The dialogue creates the alignment.

Every manager has to assess her tolerance for robust dialogue and decide how to structure participation by her group in decision making. She will weigh, and balance, several factors:

- Her personal comfort level

- The realistic requirements of the moment

- The significance of the decision to her superior and peers

- The maturity level of her subordinates

Weighing those factors, a manager will, from time to time, come down at a variety of points:

- "Team, we've got to implement this starting tomorrow morning. It's not optional. The decision has been made at corporate level. It's the end of the day and we don't even have time to talk about it. If you have feelings about it, we will have to deal with them later. Just please do it. I need you all on board."

- "Team, we need to make a decision about this. I'm not married to any foregone conclusion. In fact, I'm going to ask you to make the decision. There are many good ways we could go. It's up to you. But before we leave this room in an hour, I want your decision."

- "Team, here are the three options I'm considering as we make this decision. I'll take the responsibility to decide, but I need your input. We've got a couple of weeks so there's plenty of time for us to weigh our options."

- "What do you think?"

- "Team, I'm strongly leaning toward decision X. But I need to check and be sure I'm aware of the impact that would have. What do you see? What do you forecast if we go this way?"

The participation that fosters alignment is easier to get when the manager meets two conditions:

1. He is not driven to one of the positions almost all the time out of personality and style influences that blind him to wider considerations.

2. He is really in the position he says he is in. He doesn't claim to be in one position while really in another. When conditions outside his control require a reversal, he gives the team a thorough explanation.

Managers fostering alignment establish the boundaries within which the game will be played. Without boundaries, there is no game. Managers then invite robust participation within those boundaries.

EVERYONE HAS A TERRITORY, BUT NO ONE HAS A KINGDOM

Parkside Medical Services developed a policy that powerfully fostered alignment and nipped most alignment problems in the bud before they could come to flower. New employees, referred to as staff (as is typical in healthcare organizations), received an hour-long training session familiarizing them with this policy.

Values for Living and Working Together

1. Every staff member has a territory, but no staff member has a kingdom. Your territory is important. Some territories are larger and some contain greater responsibilities. But no one has a kingdom. Within our own territories and working together with people in other territories, we are here to provide quality care for the consumers and their families.

2. A certain degree of appropriate participatory management does exist. However, decisions have to be made by management people appropriate to their responsibilities and accountabilities.

3. There is delegation of responsibility and with that, accountability. Whenever responsibility that needs to be delegated really isn't delegated or accountability isn't being required, there are procedures to deal with that at the appropriate level.

4. Resolution of problems is to occur at the lowest level possible. For unresolved problems, the management person will be expected to initiate the process of going with the employee (or employees) to the next appropriate level. If the management person doesn't do this, the other employee (or employees) has the responsibility to request this of the manager. If the manager refuses, the employee (or employees) is to go to the next level. Obviously, the management person would be accountable for not initiating or supporting such a process.

   Management persons are oriented to this policy and procedure and its implications. We have built in assessment mechanisms to assure that all management persons are effectively communicating and practicing this policy and procedure.

Given this kind of responsibility in problem resolution, you are asked to trust that you can carry it out with no jeopardy to yourself. You will find that this process is both essential and trustworthy.

5. There are different job and responsibility levels. But there is no status rank. Every staff person is to be related with as a fellow human being. No staff person is to be perceived as being lesser or to be related to in a condescending or demeaning manner. No staff person is to be used.

6. We want your ideas. We want to know what you think would improve our work together. We want to know what you think are some of the problems that are inhibiting or negating the fulfillment of our purpose. But don't just come with problems. Bring some suggestions or possible alternatives.

7. Like the consumers, staff need support systems. If you don't experience support from other staff, we want to know about it.

8. We underscore the importance of giving fellow staff members honest praise or positive recognition.

9. Staff need the capability for self-assessment in regard to knowledge of one's strengths and limitations, realizing that both need to be affirmed and limitations don't make one less of a person. We all have our limitations.

10. Staff need to be aware of their own potential for growth and be open to learning and growth both individually and with the program.

11. For those on the treatment teams, there is the necessity of coming to understand and accept the presence, place and content of the various disciplines. Such understanding needs to be integrated into the content and practice of one's own discipline. This marks the difference between an interdisciplinary and multidisciplinary team. We cultivate the former.

(Quoted by permission from Martin Doot, M.D., former Vice President Medical Services Parkside Medical Services, Corp.)

THE TREASURE OF ALIGNMENT

The pleasure of working in an aligned organization or group is something that people never forget. I have asked thousands of people, "What was the best job you ever had, and what made it the best?" Common themes arise in their answers:

- "Well, it was my boss. She held standards high, you knew what you were expected to deliver. But that didn't keep her from being very supportive. When you screwed up, she was there to help you learn so that you didn't do it again."

- "You know, when I worked there it felt like everybody, really everybody, was on the same team. There wasn't a lot of politics and competing for advantage. There wasn't a lot of secret keeping. If someone from another unit knew something that could help you, they told you."

- "People from the President on down paid attention to the big picture. It seemed like they talked about it all the time. And when they said the company valued something, it showed up in what they expected you to do on the front line. Everything just kind of hung together. We walked the talk."

When managers build alignment, it becomes a deep well that they can draw from. On the most dry day, managers remind people of who they are—of the beauty of their alignment. It brings refreshment and new energy.

If you want to build and use the lever of alignment more naturally, here are some things you could think through and decide.

1. Look at the list of fourteen things on page 113 that great managers align. Where are the great alignments that you can acknowledge with employees? Where is there an important misalignment that you want to discuss with your group or your manager?

2. How aligned are you with your manager? On a scale of 1 – 10 (with ten being most aligned) how would you rate your alignment? What could you do to move the alignment up the scale? What do you want to do? You probably know. It is usually a matter of courage and persistence.

3. Are there smokestacks in your organization? If so, how could you start a conversation with your peers about what they are costing and the wisdom of dismantling them?

4. Decide what you will do to keep the superordinate goal at the center of attention— your attention and that of your subordinates.

5. Consider using the Thomas-Killman Conflict Mode Instrument and/or helping your unit develop a Rules of Engagement document.

6. Does the policy "Values for Living and Working Together" suggest developing a similar one in your organization?

The 7th Lever: Change

*"It is … the responsibility of the expert to operate the familiar
and that of the leader to transcend it."*

—Henry Kissinger

Great managers don't just cope with change, they lead it. This leverage ensures organizational survival in the current tumultuous environment. More than that, it takes an organization beyond survival to greatness. We are living through one of the great periods of rapid change in human history. You can put it down in your little book of eternal truths about management that you will either lead change or be its casualty. Great managers are not just caretakers. They change things.

An army of consultants, bookstores full of books on change in the business environment, and the 103 million links that came up on a recent Internet search on "change leadership" all testify to the creation of a full-blown industry bent on helping managers use this lever.

Managers attend to two major sources of change: the changes driven by large trends in the culture and the changes they see as needed within the organization.

Organizations are set down in a culture. Change drivers in the culture have enormous power: technological development, the creation of an expanding global marketplace, shifting priorities held by political decision makers, extremism married to political will and visions, shifting customer requirements in affluent and emerging economies, a more culturally diverse workforce than in the recent past, the new ability of a tiny business startup in a student's dormitory room or garage to challenge multinational corporations in a few short years.

Managers are always evaluating current operations and asking themselves if there is a faster, better, cheaper, simpler way to operate for greater efficiency and effectiveness. Skill at this level is one of the distinguishing marks of successful managers. But managers who attend to this level to the neglect of change drivers in the culture put their organization at great risk. Neglect of the big picture by a manager too fixated on the nuts and bolts is a too familiar theme. Some have called it "rearranging the deck chairs on the Titanic."

The macro-environment includes influences in the wider environment for your goods or services but which are outside the direct control of your organization. When macro-environment trends cross the boundaries of an unprepared organization, chaos and tumult result. Managers prevent this by understanding the trends and leading their organizations into creative adaptations.

Great managers monitor both the macro-environment and the micro-environment in which their organization operates—the big picture and the small picture. Some managers fall prey to a narrow view. They stay fixated on day-to-day challenges. They lose sight of the large trends and influences outside the organization that suggest great opportunity or threat to viability. Great managers, even those not at the most senior level, maintain their curiosity about ways the macro-environment could affect their organizations. If you are not in the top ranks of management, there is no better way to demonstrate your value to upper management than to show that you have the ability to understand both the macro and micro dimensions of your organization's life.

Managers work to anticipate influential changes in the macro-environment and lead changes in the organization that will avoid loss and maximize opportunity.

LEADERSHIP UPSETS STABILITY

Human nature longs for stability and resists change. Organizations resist change. It is hard to abandon what has worked before. We resist upsetting comfortable security. Organizations can become victims of their own success. Doing pretty well can blind organizations and managers to both peril and extraordinary opportunity. Responding to the human tendency to resist change, John Wesley, founder of The United Methodist Church, told his ministers that their job was not only to comfort the afflicted, but also to afflict the comfortable.

> Everything in the world wants to be mediocre. It is only by caring for excellence, and by an act of will, that change for the better comes about. Great managers bring that care and will to the organizational dance.

Very early in a change process, a manager must use the voice of leadership to upset comfortable fixed perceptions. Leveraging stability toward change is difficult. It is anxiety provoking. The first anxiety is the manager's. Sometimes you may wonder if those hearing your call for change will "kill the messenger" rather than absorb the message.

Launching change processes usually requires a manager to afflict the comfortable. The bad news, the urgency for change, must precede the good news. What will be the cost of not changing? Why upset good enough? What peril will the organization encounter unless changes are made? How is that likely to affect the organization, units and individual employees?

Even if a manager's direct reports are not asking these questions, an effective manager will answer them and create and appropriate level of anxiety.

The voice of leadership says:

- The environment for our goods and services is changing in ways that are significant for us. Unless we make significant changes we will be left behind. The cost will be _____. We can't afford to pay that price.

- Here are the changes I see that we must make

- If we can do this, and I believe we can, great opportunities are going to open up. A preferred and possible future is at our doorstep.

- Let's go!

MANAGERSHIP SHOWS THE WAY

Anxiety has the ability to launch action or to paralyze it. Managers leading change processes measure the level of a group's anxiety. They create felt discomfort with the status quo. But in order to not paralyze the group, the manager holds the attitude and models the behavior that says, "We can do this. Let's look together and think through the best way to get it done. Here's what I see. What do you think? What could stand in our way? What could make it more doable?"

Great managers contain their anxiety and do not telegraph it to the people they lead. That doesn't mean minimizing the challenges. It means that the manager tells the truth, but frames it in such a way that the truth does not become demoralizing. "This is an uphill pull gang. But we're the A-team. We've risen to challenges before. It's who we are. So what we need to talk about is how we're going to meet this challenge. We don't have time for a lot of commiserating about it. What are your ideas? How are we going to get this done?"

Here is a way to engage a group in the robust dialogue that gets people on board with a change initiative. I have used it successfully and taught it to a great many managers:

1. Ask your group to define the change that is being launched in one to three sentences that are crystal clear. Write their description on a paper flip chart.

2. Distribute small pieces of paper and ask everyone to write a number on the page indicating their attitude about launching the change, using the following key:

   1. No way. I won't go.

   2. Probably not. I'd have to be convinced.

   3. Maybe. I'm not sure.

   4. OK. Let's give it a try.

   5. Absolutely. This is great! Let's go.

3. Collect and summarize the numbers on the flip chart:

   • Number of people who entered each number (1 – 5)

   • Average of all the submissions

4. Ask the group this question: "What would you have to know, what would you have to feel, and what would you have to do to move up one number higher than the one you wrote on your slip of paper?"

They will tell you. Because you have created a safe ritual of engagement, they will tell you what they need to tell you. Their answers tell you what you need to be talking about with them.

Offering an encounter like this is an act of faith by a manager. It is an act of faith in employees—faith that they have the capacity, if given the opportunity, to participate at this level. Even more fundamentally, it is an act of faith in oneself. A manager struggling toward this affirmation of faith in himself said, "Good night! If I open this can of worms, who knows where it will go? I may never be able to get things headed in the direction we need to go."

Yes, there is risk. A manager who's willing to run the risk of contrary opinions will find that facilitating discussion of those opinions is the royal road to team cohesion. And there are no effective change processes without team cohesion.

Working groups called to make significant change are between a rock and a hard place. Let the rock stand for the dread of the consequences of not changing, and the hard place stand for the dread of change.

The concept of being "between a rock and a hard place" originated in Greek mythology with the phrase, "between Scylla and Charybdis." Scylla was a horribly grotesque monster living in a rock that endangered sailors on one side of the Straits of Messina. On the other side of the strait was Charybdis, another sea monster, that, taking the form of a whirlpool, devoured anything within range.

Navigating culture change in an organization is something like being in the Straits of Messina. Anxiety for the comfortable lost past on one side, and anxiety over the unknown future on the other. Managers sensitive to this will signal an understanding of both anxieties and the opportunity that lurks in the uncertainty.

The voice of management says:

- That's the vision for the future that will be created by the major changes our organization is going to make. Let's talk about how to best get it done in our unit.

- What will make it possible for us to execute this change? What could pull the rug out from under our efforts to change?

- Here's what I believe we can do. What do you see?

- You're the "A Team." Let's go!

When the contemplated change is major, the manager with a mid-sized or large group cannot carry this message alone. The manager in this situation enlists others in the unit to help develop the critical mass required to tip the balance and execute the change. This manager needs a smaller group he can enlist to be a change driving team with him.

He will want to select this group carefully, recruiting people who:

- Are entirely on board and committed to the change process

- Have credibility with their peers

- Talk a lot

Managers enlist the change-driving team by:

- Talking with them individually or in a small group, explaining the anticipated change thoroughly

- Spending adequate time responding to questions and any misgivings

- Describing how they can function on the change-driving team by informally backing the change and helping explain it to others

- Indicating continuing availability to them to support them in the role

- Asking for a yes or no—will they help in this way?

CHANGES THAT IMPACT THE ORGANIZATION'S CULTURE

Organizations have a cultural identity. Managers want to understand the culture of their organization and its effect on behaviors and outcomes.

> "Culture is the invisible force behind the tangibles and observables in any organization, a social energy that moves people to act. Culture is to the organization what personality is to the individual—a hidden, yet unifying theme that provides meaning, direction, and mobilization … shared philosophies, ideologies, values, beliefs, assumptions, and norms. These are seldom written down or discussed, but they are learned by living in the organization and becoming a part of it."—Kilmann et al.

Managers and their groups can bring their culture to consciousness by asking three questions:

1. **What is it like to work here? How do you feel being a part of this group?**

   - Safe, valued, trusted, supported, encouraged (and sometimes prodded) to develop, accountable?

   - Unsure, discounted, anxious?

2. **What are the broadly shared assumptions that steer the organization? Assumptions about:**

   - Shared values that steer decisions?

   - The place of the organization in the broad national culture and its probable future?

   - The needs of customers, employees, suppliers—all stakeholders?

3. **How are things done around here?**

   - Who can you speak to? Who can you challenge? Are there things you can't talk about?

   - Behaviors and attitudes that people are expected to demonstrate?

   - Rewards for following norms of expected behaviors and penalties for violating them?

Changes that impact the organization's cultural identity are especially challenging and require unusual sensitivity from the manager. The culture of an organization or a unit is the ground on which people stand. Their roots go deep in that ground.

Some changes are not so significant for the culture of the organization. New policies are issued; procedures used to perform traditional tasks are revised; new equipment or technology is brought in resulting in a need for retraining; and many other modifications of how the organization works are made.

Changes that impact and bid to change the culture in significant ways usually encounter more resistance and require longer to accomplish. They are not just about how the organization performs. They touch the identity of the organization. Individuals and organizations defend their well-established identities.

Other illustrations:

- An organization that has had a history of generous benefits for employees begins to pare them back

- A company becomes unionized

- A small family-run business that has grown sells to a large company

- A hostile takeover and consequent reorganization threatens significant layoffs

- A new CEO and senior management team comes in and has a very different management style than the group that led for the last fifteen years

Managers assisting groups through large, culture-impacting change can help by presenting a unified field theory of the meaning underlying the change. The concept of a unified field theory comes from Einstein's quest in physics. There, it is an attempt to unify all the forces and the interactions between elementary particles into a single theoretical framework that would explain the nature and behavior of all matter. It is sometimes referred to as the TOE (theory of everything) and is the holy grail that physicists seek.

The virtue of a TOE used by a manager is that it conveys meaning. Meaning reduces anxiety. People sustain effort when the meaning of the effort is clear and coincides with their values. Change leaders manage meaning. They say, "The times are challenging, but here's what it's all about. And here are our choices."

Painful transitions are better tolerated, and cause less disruption, when their meaning is understood and choices are made clear. The more complex and powerful the cross-currents of change in an organization, the greater the opportunity for managers to voice the meaning of the change in understandable terms—to name and explain for followers a unified field theory. Managers who do this achieve extraordinary influence. Great managers are great explainers.

The theory that supports understanding of what is happening during massive, culture-modifying change is best conveyed in the form of a story. Managers tell the story of the organization and their unit in it. They tell the story of where the organization has been, of what it used to be, of how things evolved, of where the organization is headed now and of the chance for greatness.

What empowers leadership storytelling are not the facts of the story, not the recounting of sequential history. What empowers the storytelling are the values the story speaks of, the meanings they convey, the implied connections and the bridges they build to the future.

Hear the difference:

- The King died. A year later the Queen died.

  That is not a story. It's just facts.

- The King died. A year later, to the day, grieving her heart out, the Queen died.

  That is a story. It has meaning, states values and implies connection.

When we asked new employees what part of their two-day first-phase orientation they found most helpful, the great majority of them said it was the presentation of the CEO. When we asked them what was helpful about it, they said that he had told them the story of the organization. He had set the story in the larger context of the history of the industry, described the cultural changes that were taking place, gave hints of the next chapters in the story and provided a vision of how they had opportunity to participate in the continuing story. And, most importantly, he modeled and communicated the meanings, the values, the principles of what the organization was about.

The result? People joined up. They signed in. They got on board. As one of them wrote on his evaluation, "His feeling for the organization helped me. I'm not sure how, but I'm glad to be here."

Managers look for ways of telling the story that will cause people to say, "Yes, I see what all this is about. It isn't going to be easy, but it's worth working for … I'll get (or stay) on board."

Stories have a beginning, a middle, an end and a meaning. The master outline for many of the great stories that great managers tell looks like this:

- This is who we were

- This is what we are going through

- This where we're going

- This is why it is important and why we are going to be successful

The story carries simple clarity to the hundred things that are pressuring an organization going through culture change. Great managers tell the story and convey confidence. They brace themselves, touch again the bedrock of their confidence and use the voice of leadership to make the changes understandable. They know and feel the uncertainties and contingencies that shape the future. But they say to those they lead, "Trust me—we're going somewhere worth going." Courage is the price and the fuel of leadership.

MOVING AHEAD

Once the urgency to change is felt and the meanings understood, managers continue to move the process forward. Much of the work involves answering questions—those who are asked and those who are not. You can get a feel for the questions and concerns by imagining what Christopher Columbus and his crew must have gone through …

Columbus' ships are leaving Europe for the new world tomorrow. Lying in their bunks, what questions do you think the crews are asking themselves?

- Should I really go through with this?

- Does Chris really know what he is doing? Is he crazy?

- Do we have the wherewithal to see it through? Will the food and water hold out?

- Will we fall off the edge of the earth? I've seen those maps.

- Will the sea monsters get us?

Weeks later, they are mid-journey and appear to be going nowhere.

- How long can this go on? Is there no end to it?
- Can we turn back?
- Why did we embark on such a useless enterprise? It wasn't so bad back home.

More weeks later, someone climbs the mast, looks West and cries out, "Land!"

- What will this new place be like?
- Will it be all we were promised?
- Will the people be friendly or hostile?
- How will I sustain myself in new ways?

This fantasy reminds managers that as the change process extends over time they must answer the new questions that come up and maintain the urgency.

They say, "We are not there yet, but we have made gains and are headed in the right direction." If this is not to sound hollow and breed mistrust, it must confirm people's own impressions. The talk must make reference to shared experience, not fantasy. It can't be faked. A manager will take pains to create, and acknowledge, successes that move a group partway toward the eventual goal. Human nature cannot sustain an eighteen-month change process without seeing some gains along the way.

Training in the United States Army includes a legendary hike of many miles that tests endurance and stress levels as reflected in biological changes. The research showed that when the troops were not informed, or misinformed along the way of how far they had come and how much further they had to go, stress levels were high. But when the troops were accurately and regularly informed of mileposts indicating progress, stress levels were reduced.

Managers leveraging change celebrate small wins along the way: "We survived that storm last night, and isn't it beautiful today? Good work! We eat meat tonight."

Change drains energy. Celebration renews it.

CONSOLIDATING

There comes a tipping point when it is clear to everyone that there is no going back. Everything is not done, but much is. The group comes to know that now both feet are in the new reality, even when they glance back over their shoulder occasionally.

Managers facilitate entry into this stage of change by being the first to recognize its leading edge and naming it. They describe what has changed: "This is how we work now, and it's working well."

They show what has not changed: "We will be OK in this new place. The same skills that let us thrive back there will serve us here. This is how we function now. We are in a new place. We have new ways. But we still have our grounding in the core values that make us who we are."

Managers leveraging change are prepared to change everything except the core values—theirs and the company's.

Here are some things you could do to become better prepared to use the lever of change.

1. List three changes in structures or processes that if you could wave a magic wand you would change immediately to make your unit more effective.

2. Now that you have named them, make some notes about how you would take the first steps to:

   - Raise an appropriate level of anxiety

   - More clearly define the shape and benefits of your proposed changes

   - Secure the input and backing of your manager

   - Enlist change drivers

   - Launch the change

   - Continue to move the change forward to completion

3. What changes do you see coming in the environment for your goods or services that could significantly affect how your organization and unit need to change? Hold this discussion with some of your peers and your manager.

4. Do you identify gaps between the espoused core values of your organization and its culture? If so, think through how you might take positive steps to start closing the gap. Who should you talk with?

5. Think through how you can better explain the meaning of the changes your organization is going through to the people you lead.

The Fulcrum

In order to achieve its power, a lever must be placed on a fulcrum—a point of support on which a lever tips. Archimedes is usually pictured resting a lever on a rock—a fulcrum. The fulcrum transfers the force applied on one end of the lever to the other where the weight is lifted.

There is a fulcrum that makes every lever we have considered effective. Your character is the fulcrum—your integrity, your judgment, your trustworthiness, your feeling of legitimacy in the role of manager. These things create an internal state of thinking and feeling that causes people to move toward you and with you rather than away from or against you.

Personal readiness to lead gives the levers an effective fulcrum. Your strengths will render your weaknesses unimportant.

Managerial effectiveness is about:

- Character and competence
- Building confidence and coaching
- Building a motivational environment and structure for work that is worthy of people's best contribution
- Modeling the behavior you want to see in others

Who taught you to walk? You probably began to do it when you were about one year old. Who taught you to do that? Nobody. You saw the big people doing it and you wanted it. It works that way in organizational life. Managers walk. People see.

I don't know what you aspire to, and I don't know what your gifts are. It takes some of us a long time to discover our gifts. Identify your best strength and pursue it. Do more of it. Do it every day. Find what you love and work hard to become as good at it as you can possibly be. Commit yourself to continuous continuous (yes, the repeated word is not a typographical error) improvement.

Exceptional intelligence does not guarantee extraordinary accomplishment. Neither does working to overcome deficiencies. Instead, commit to two or three strengths and develop them. Your strengths can probably be discovered in:

- *Your wants.* What do you really want? Powerfully want? There is probably a strength there.

- *Your pleasures.* What do you get a kick out of doing? What really fulfills you? What do you go home feeling good about? If it doesn't feel good, it is probably not a strength. If it does, it probably is.

- *What you learn easily.* If you pick up a new learning or skill quickly, it probably reflects a strength. Subjectively it feels like, "Oh, yeah, I know that."

- *What you naturally do well.* There come times when you just know that you are doing a great job. It is flowing easily. Athletes call it being "in the zone." When you don't have to work hard to do it, it probably is a strength.

Action Steps You Can Take

Finish this sentence. My two best strengths are …

_____

and _____

It is likely that you want to be a leader/manager because you have read this far. Whether or not you currently are developing the strengths that support the practice of management, there are a few things that will aid your search and development:

- Read the best leadership and management books that you can find, but these alone will not grant you the ways of great managers

- Attend the best training you can find, but training alone will not give you what Tom Wolfe, in his novel about astronauts selected for the NASA space program, called *The Right Stuff.*

- Spend time with a mentor, coach or great manager who will model the way and help you take it. But no one else can take you from where you are to where you want to go.

- Turn inward where the act of creation is taking place and see if you are coming to love this kind of work

These great contributors to your career in management can help you take up the levers. But the fulcrum point rests in who you are. I once knew a manager whose most influential thing was her laughter. No matter how challenging the day, people would hear her laughter and feel reassured. Her laughter said, "We will be OK. These are times of testing, but that's alright. We are people of spirit and that spirit will sustain us through any storm." She didn't often say those things directly. She didn't have to. Her laughter said them.

This manager didn't figure this out as a management strategy. She didn't go to a training workshop on laughter as a tool of leadership. She didn't have to. When you become a manager, there you are, in all of your individuality, "Warts and all," as Churchill said. People see. People hear.

An actress friend told me that the best acting classes she has taken, with some very high-powered and expensive coaches, are very personal. Acting comes down to who you are, and being able to reach down into yourself to project who you are. If you are playing the part of a Queen, you have to find that in yourself that wants to be Queen. If you are playing the part of a deceiver, you have to find that in yourself that has been deceitful. Otherwise, it's just role-playing. And the audience knows the difference. It's the same way for managers. What you are doing had better resonate with who you are.

Don Bennett was the first amputee to climb Mt. Rainier—14,410 feet on one leg and two crutches. He was interviewed later, and the interviewer asked him why he wanted to be the first amputee to climb Mt. Rainier. Don said it was because he wanted to demonstrate to other people that they were capable of doing more than they might have thought they could do. It wasn't just about him. He had a vision of others doing great things.

That's a pretty good metaphor for great management—helping others rise to their capacities and do great things.

Perhaps you are ready to follow the model presented in *The Leadership Challenge* to:

- Model the passion, the will and the behavior that can take others to the top of their potential

- Inspire a shared vision of a possible and preferred future for an organization

- Challenge and change structures and processes so that the same amount of effort will leverage to greater results

You know who you are, and the people you lead will need to know three things about you:

1. **They need to know that you know the product or service.** If you have worked on the front line providing the product or service, you gain credibility. If you have not, you will find other ways of learning and demonstrating your knowledge.

2. **They need to know that you belong in leadership.** They come to know this as they witness your integrity, as they see you meet challenges successfully, and as you build their self-confidence.

3. **They need to know that you are enjoying yourself.** This is not a matter of spreading happy talk. They will know if you are not overburdened, not discouraged. Maintain your love of the mission, product or service. Don't let it be crushed by everydayness. The people you lead will know if even when the challenge is most steep, you are empowered by hope. And they will not only know. They will catch your spirit.

Enjoy the journey!

REFERENCES

Albrecht, Karl. *Social Intelligence—The New Science of Success*, San Francisco: Jossey-Bass, 2006.

Bennis, Warren. *On Becoming a Leader.* Reading, Massachusetts: Addison-Wesley Publishing Company, 1989.

Block, Peter. *The Empowered Manager,* San Francisco: Jossey-Bass, 1987.

Clarke, Boyd, and Ron Crossland. *The Leader's Voice.* New York: Select Books, 2002.

Collins, Jim. *Good to Great.* New York: HarperCollins, 2001.

Covey, Stephen R. "Beyond the Performance Review." *Chief Learning Officer,* August 2005, 22.

Covey, Stephen R. *The 7 Habits of Highly Effective People.* New York: Simon and Schuster, 1989.

Kilmann, Ralph H., Mary J. Saxton, Roy Serpa and Associates. *Gaining Control of the Corporate Culture.* San Francisco: Jossey-Bass Publishers, 1990.

Kotter, John P. *Leading Change.* Boston: Harvard Business School Press, 1996.

Kouzes, James M. and Barry Z. Posner. *The Leadership Challenge,* 4th Edition. New York: John Wiley & Sons, Inc., 2007.

Lencioni, Patrick. *Overcoming the Five Dysfunctions of a Team.* San Francisco: Jossey-Bass, 2005.

McGregor, Douglas. T*he Human Side of Enterprise—Annotated Edition.* New York: McGraw-Hill Companies, 2006.

Nelson, Bob, Ken Blanchard and Stephen Schudlich. *1001 Ways to Reward Employees.* New York: Workman Publishing, 1994.

Palmer, Parker J. "Leading From Within." *Insights On Leadership*, in Larry C. Spears (ed.). New York: John Wiley & Sons, Inc., 1998, 197 – 208.

Spreier, Scott W., Mary H. Fontaine and Ruth L. Malloy. "Leadership Run Amok—The Destructive Potential of Overachievers." *Harvard Business Review*: June 2006, 72 – 82.

Welch, Jack. *Winning.* New York: HarperCollins, 2005.